EASY ORIGAMI

ANIMALS

400 PAGES READY TO FOLD WITH 10 STEP-BY-STEP TUTORIALS

GUILLAUME DENIS

DAVID & CHARLES
— PUBLISHING —

www.davidandcharles.com

A DAVID AND CHARLES BOOK

61, Boulevard Saint-Germain
75240 Paris Cedex 05
www.editions-eyrolles.com

David and Charles is an imprint of David and Charles, Ltd
Suite A, Tourism House, Pynes Hill, Exeter, EX2 5WS

First published in the UK and USA in 2025
Content originally published in France as *Origami Volume 1: Les Bases* in 2018 and *Origami Volume 2: Techniques Avancées* in 2021

A catalogue record for this book is available from the British Library.

ISBN-13: 9781446316405 paperback

This book has been printed on paper from approved suppliers and made from pulp from sustainable sources.

Printed in China through Asia Pacific Offset for:
David and Charles, Ltd
Suite A, Tourism House, Pynes Hill, Exeter, EX2 5WS

10 9 8 7 6 5 4 3 2 1

Publishing Director: Ame Verso
Senior Commissioning Editor: Nigel Browning
Publishing Manager: Jeni Chown
Project Editor: Cheryl Brown
Editorial Assistant: Jenna McGill
Lead Designer: Sam Staddon
Junior Designer: Giulia Sandri
Pre-press Designer: Susan Reansbury
Illustrations: Guillaume Denis
Production Manager: Beverley Richardson

David and Charles publishes high-quality books on a wide range of subjects. For more information visit www.davidandcharles.com.

Share your makes with us on social media using #dandcbooks and follow us on Facebook and Instagram by searching for @dandcbooks.

CONTENTS

FOLDS AND SYMBOLS

Before you begin, study the following information carefully. It sets out all of the basic folds you will need to make the origami models in this book.

Each fold and its movement is represented on a diagram by an arrow and the angle of the fold to be made is indicated with a broken line. To avoid any errors, make sure you know the difference between "folding the paper" and "marking the fold". In the first case, the paper stays folded. In the second you fold it and unfold it as indicated by the double arrow.

Don't worry if your folds aren't perfect at first! The 400 sheets of paper will let you practice folding, unfolding, assembling and making any number of amazing creations.

PAPER COLOR CHOICE

The designs can be made with a plain sheet of paper, the same on both sides, but if you choose a piece that's different on each side, the start position of the paper is important so follow the symbols to make sure it's the right-side up before folding.

Two-tone, main color beneath

Two-tone, main color on top

White plain sheet

Colored plain sheet

TYPES OF FOLD

There are many different folds, which are really just the combination of the two basic folds: the valley fold and the mountain fold. The broken lines indicate the nature of a fold: short dashes for the hollow valley and long dashes and dots for the raised mountain. Since a sheet has two sides, valley fold and mountain fold are just opposite aspects of one and the same fold. When we talk about valley fold or mountain fold, it is always in relation to the face of the paper.

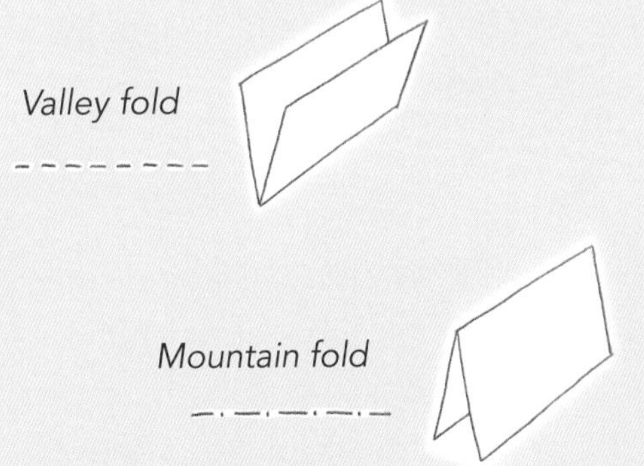

MOVEMENT ARROWS

The arrows indicate the movement that will form the fold (movement in front or movement behind) as well as its direction (up, down, left, etc.). Associated with the two types of broken lines which indicate the position and nature of the fold (valley fold and mountain fold), they provide us with precise information on the creation of these two basic folds.

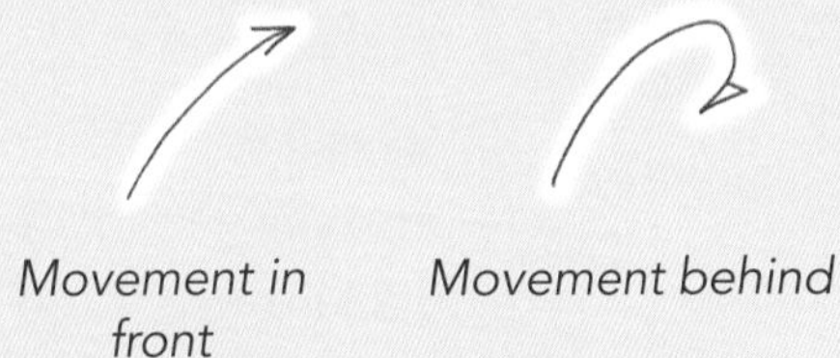

ADDING DETAILS

Where a model is finished with a pencil or felt-tip pen, for those final animal-defining decorative touches, this symbol makes it clear, although stickers could just as easily be used.

SYMBOL KEY

FOLD Make a fold in this direction.

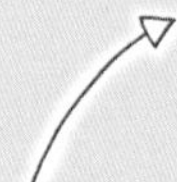

UNFOLD Unfold in this direction.

FOLD AND UNFOLD Mark a fold by folding and unfolding it.

MARKED FOLD An unfolded fold leaves a mark called a "marked fold". It is represented by a thin line, whereas the edges of the paper are shown with a thicker line.

TURN OVER Flip your model over to the other side, so that what was on the bottom is now on top.

ROTATE The model must be rotated in the direction of the arrows.

PRESS This little black triangle can mean "to press", or "to push in", or "to flatten" so follow the instructions carefully.

HOLD HERE This circle indicates the part of the paper to hold to carry out the action described.

BLOW This means "inflate by blowing here".

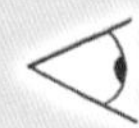

VIEWPOINT CHANGES This indicates that the angle at which the model is viewed has changed, e.g. from side to front view.

ENLARGED VIEW This indicates that the next diagram is shown at a larger scale than the ones that came before.

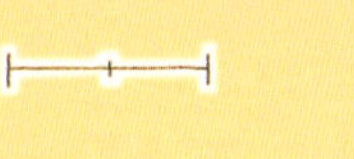

EQUAL SEGMENTS This symbol indicates that segments are equal to each other.

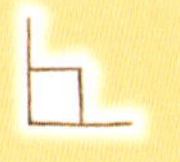

RIGHT ANGLE This symbol represents a right angle, i.e. a 90° angle.

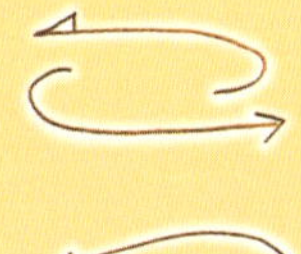

ROTATE THE FLAPS Using arrows in this configuration means "rotate the flaps around the axis as shown", and the number and arrangement of the different flaps is often clearly shown.

PLEAT FOLD This zigzag symbol indicates that a pleat fold – a combination of a mountain fold and a valley fold – is required. The quantity indicates how many paper layers to work the fold through.

REPEAT HERE Repeat the action at the indicated location.

REPEAT BEHIND Repeat the action at the indicated location at the back of the model.

REPEAT SEVERAL TIMES The number of bars are equal to the number of times that the action must be repeated.

PiG

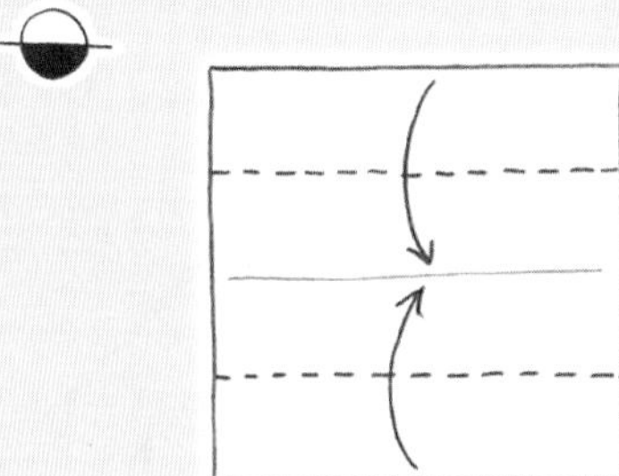

- 1 -

Fold the paper in half, then unfold to mark the center line. Fold the top and bottom edges to the center crease.

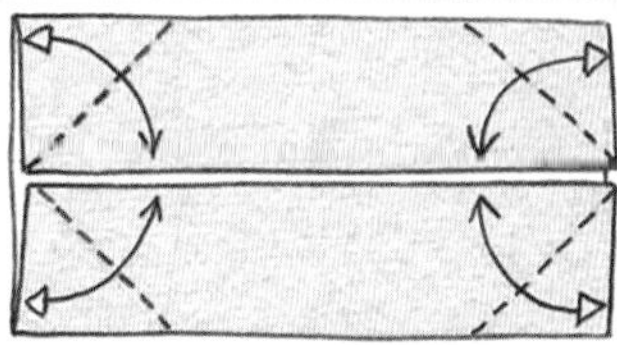

- 2 -

Fold all four corners inward along diagonal lines to meet at the center crease, then unfold.

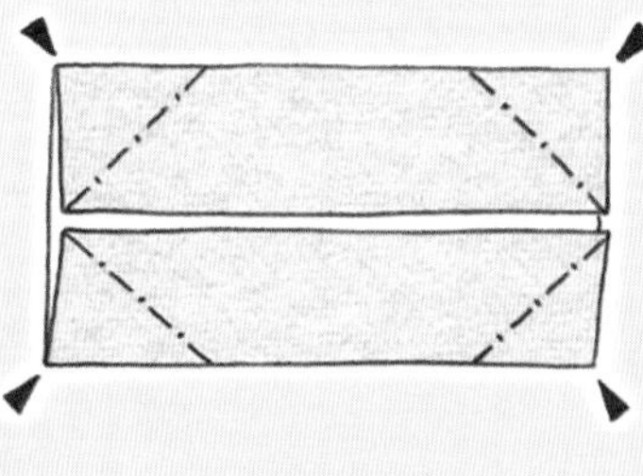

- 3 -

Push in at the marked points to fold the corners to the inside.

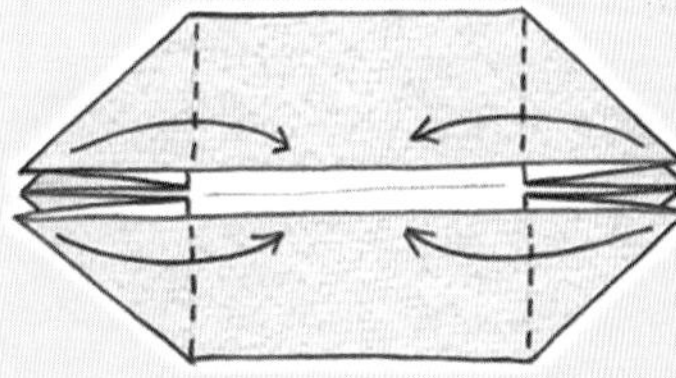

- 4 -

Fold out the top layer at each corner along the fold lines shown and flatten.

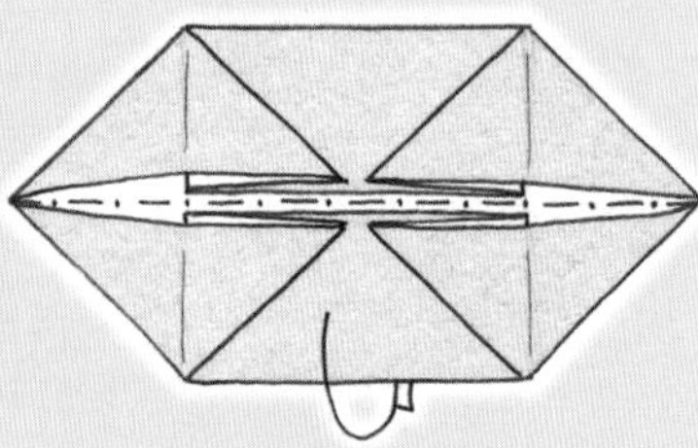

- 5 -

Fold the model in half behind, along the center crease.

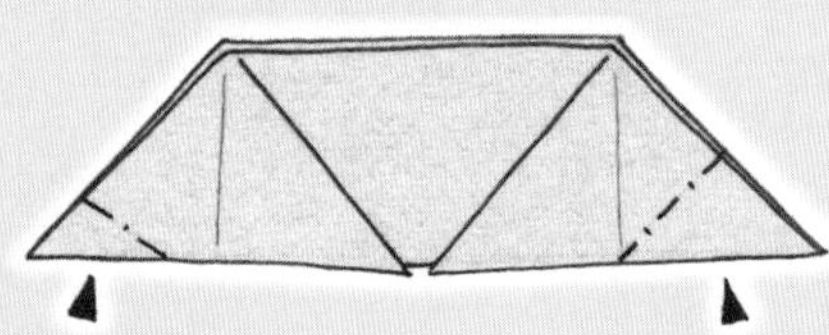

- 6 -

Push in at the marked points, folding along the indicated lines, noticing how the angle of these lines is not the same.

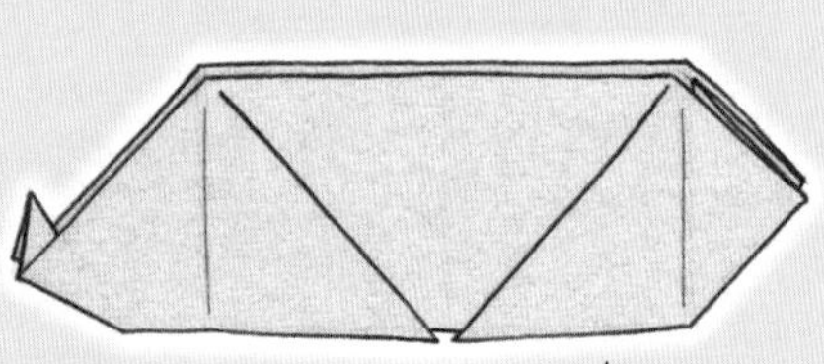

- 7 -

Flatten the model, ensuring that the creases are all sharp and precise. The pig now has a snout (left-hand side as shown).

- 8 -

Place your finger inside the right-hand side of the model to locate the inner flap (interior view shown). Push outward on the marked point, folding along the indicated line.

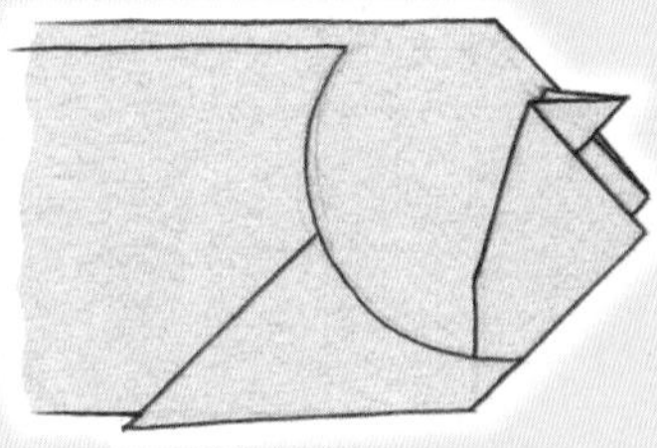

- 9 -

This creates the small triangular shape that is the tail (interior view shown).

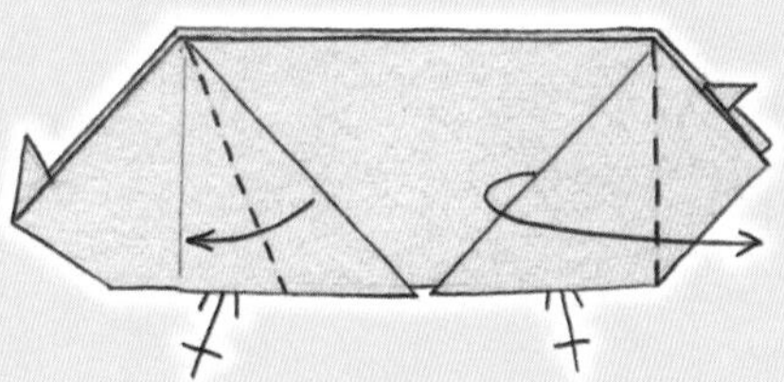

- 10 -

Fold the central flaps outward along the indicated lines. Repeat on the reverse side.

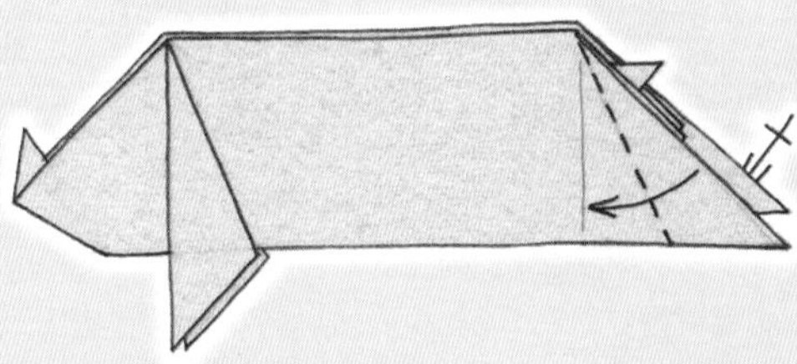

- 11 -

To complete the rear end, fold the outer flap inward as shown to create the back leg and reveal the pig's bottom. Repeat on the reverse side.

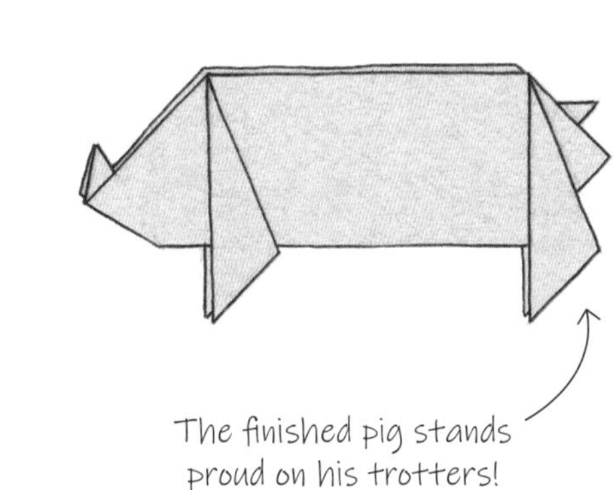

The finished pig stands proud on his trotters!

CAT

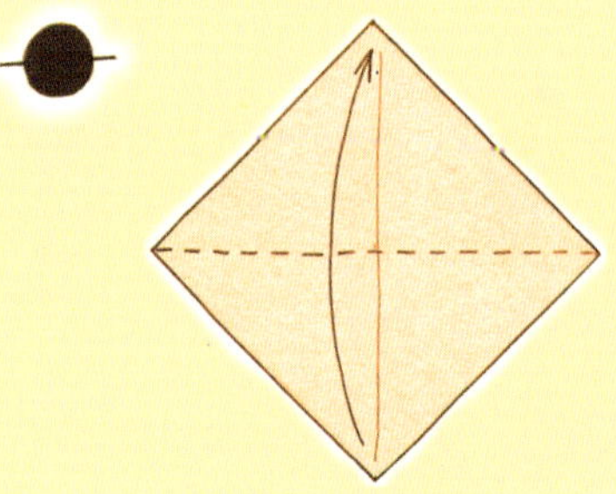

- 1 -

Fold from side to side to mark the center crease and unfold. Fold from bottom to top to make a triangle.

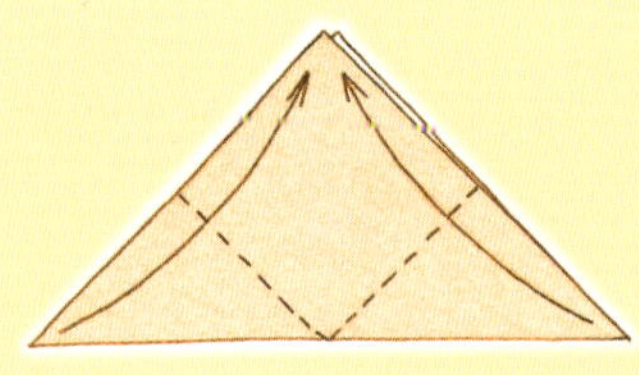

- 2 -

Fold each corner to the top.

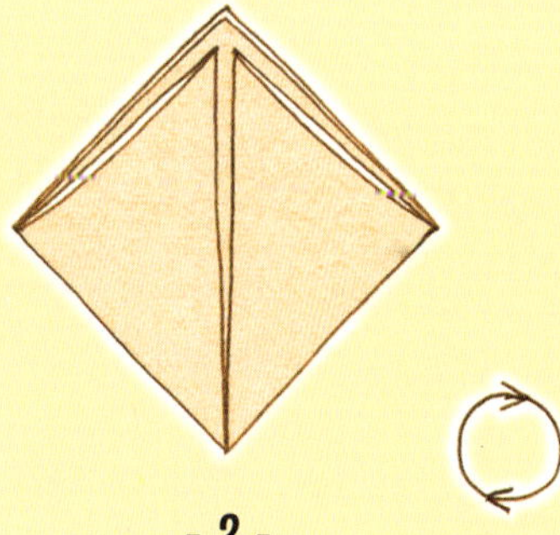

- 3 -

Your model now looks like this. Before continuing, rotate it so that the open ends are at the bottom.

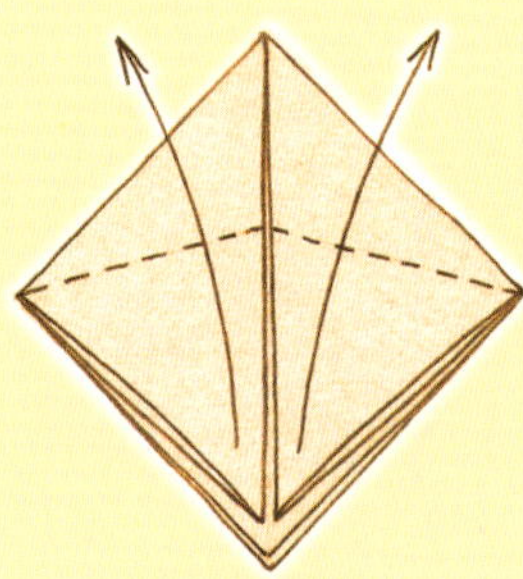

- 4 -

Fold the flaps upward and crease along the indicated lines.

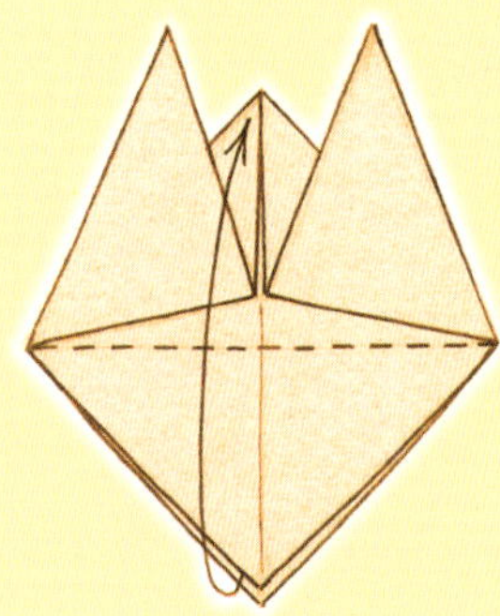

- 5 -

Fold the top layer of the bottom flap along the center crease.

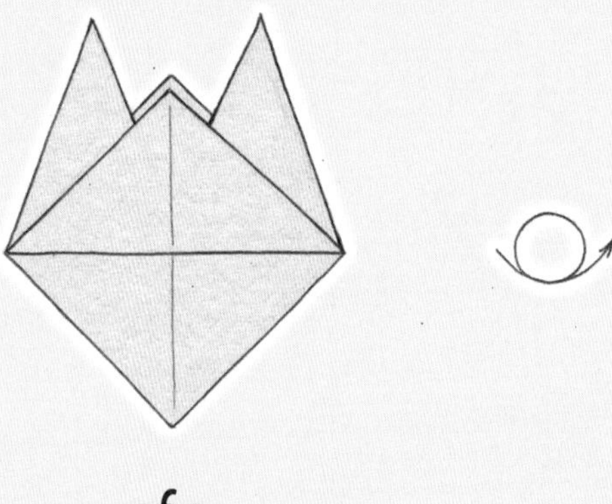

- 6 -

Your model now looks like this. Turn it over.

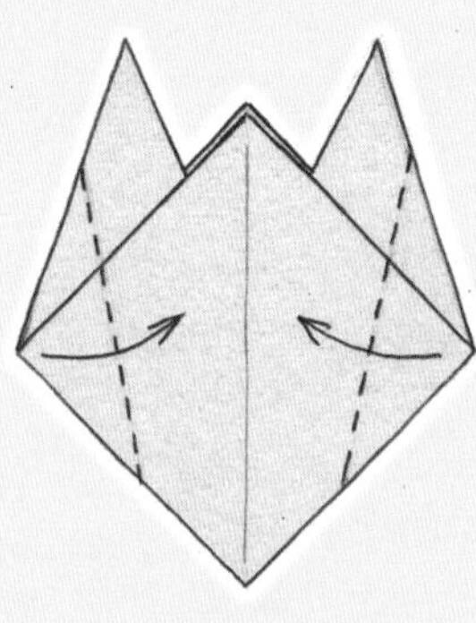

- 7 -

Fold in at the sides along the indicated lines and crease well.

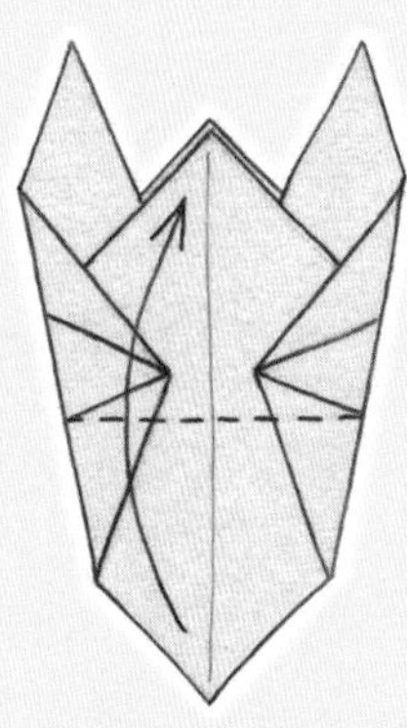

- 8 -

Fold up the bottom half to match the top half (angles of side folds may need adjustment).

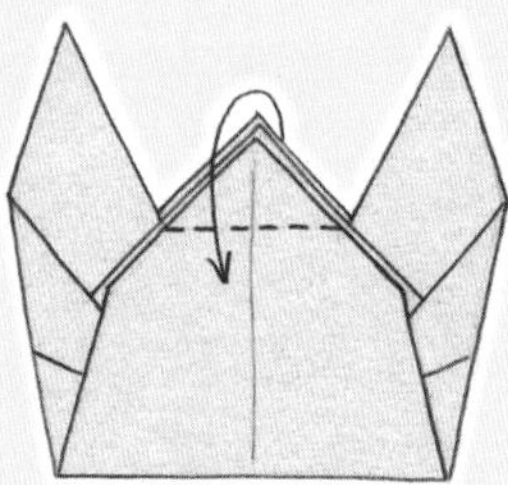

- 9 -

Fold center top point down and crease really well to make sure it stays in place.

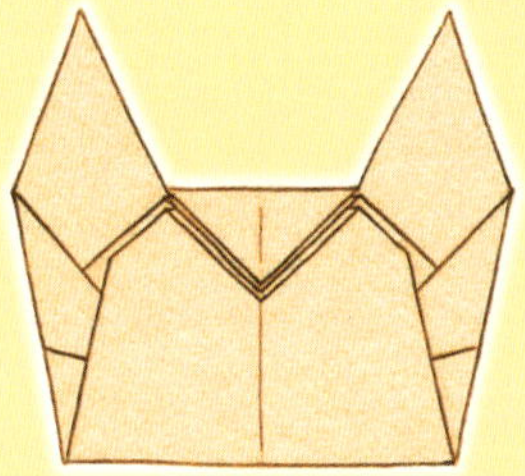

- 10 -

Your model now looks like this. Turn it over to give you the front of the cat's head.

- 11 -

There is an opening at the base of the head so that you can pop it on your finger to make a finger puppet.

Bring your cat's personality to life by using pens to draw on facial details.

ELEPHANT

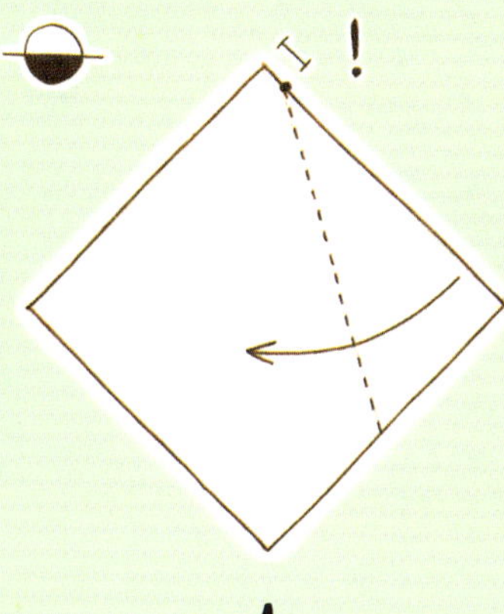

- 1 -

With paper placed as here, fold inward from one side slightly off from the top point (see !), matching the angle of the fold as shown.

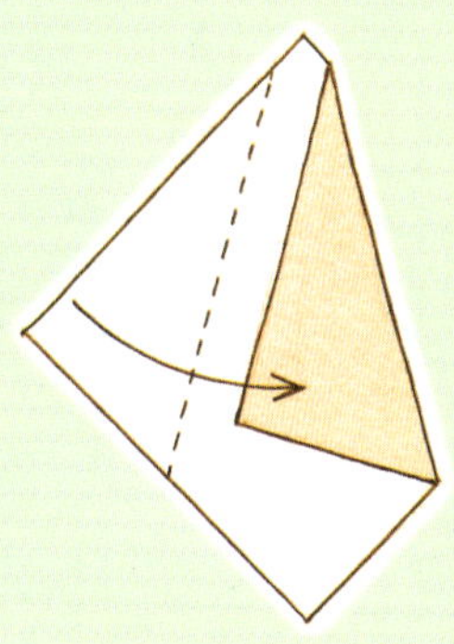

- 2 -

Repeat to fold the opposite side in. Mirroring is important throughout to achieve an elephant with perfectly even ears and tusks.

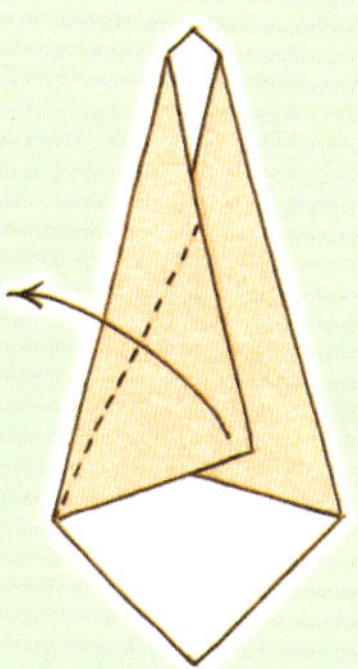

- 3 -

Fold the top flap outward as indicated.

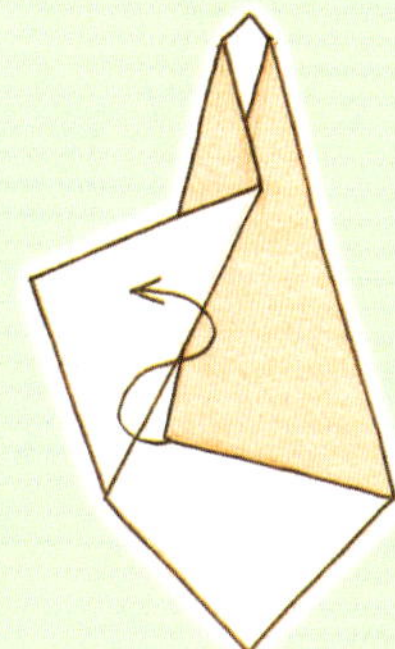

- 4 -

Bring the opposite flap over the flap just folded.

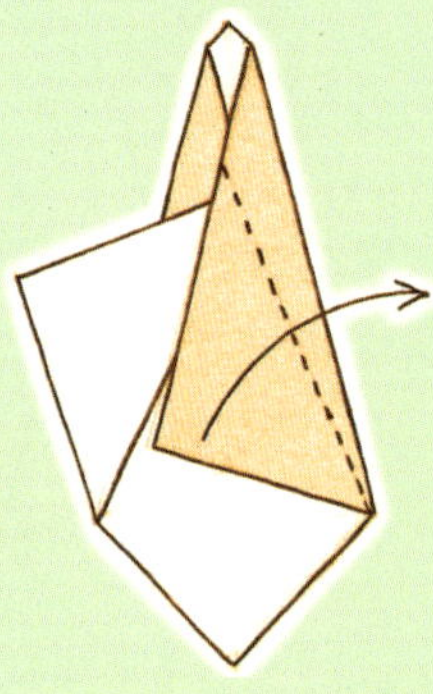

- 5 -

Then fold this flap outward matching the angle of the fold in Step 3.

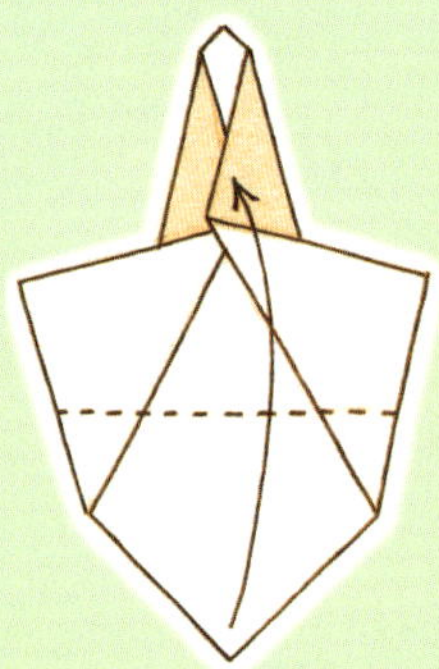

- 6 -

Fold the bottom point toward the top half, taking care to match the view seen in Step 7.

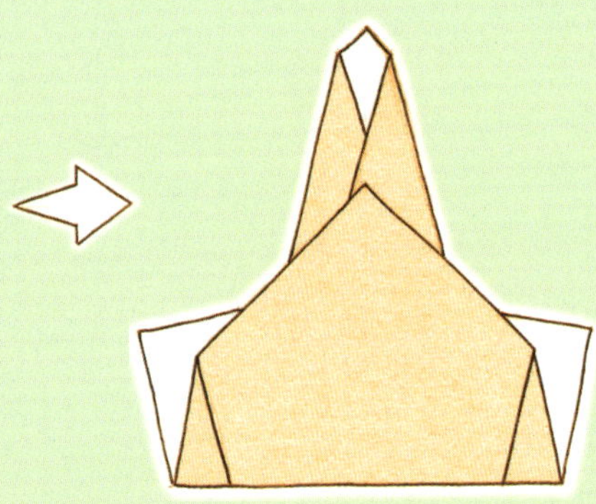

- 7 -

Your model should look like this. Turn it over and rotate it so the elephant's trunk is pointing downward.

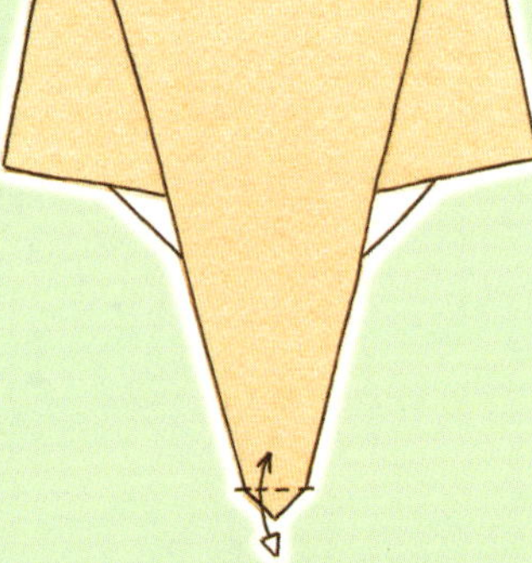

- 8 -

Fold the tip of the trunk up as indicated, then unfold.

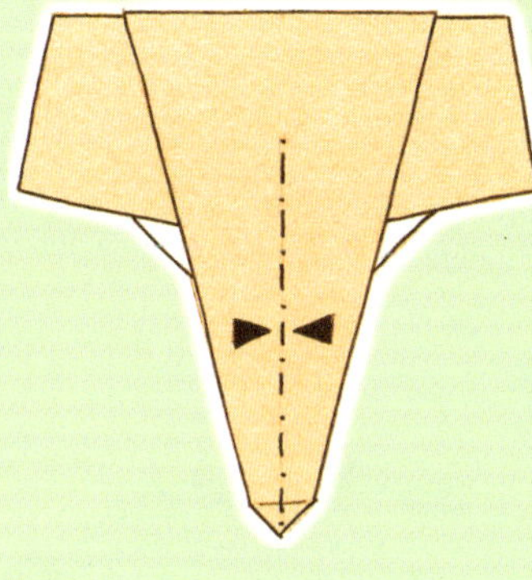

- 9 -

Starting about one-quarter of the way down from the top of the head, begin to pinch a fold along the center of the trunk.

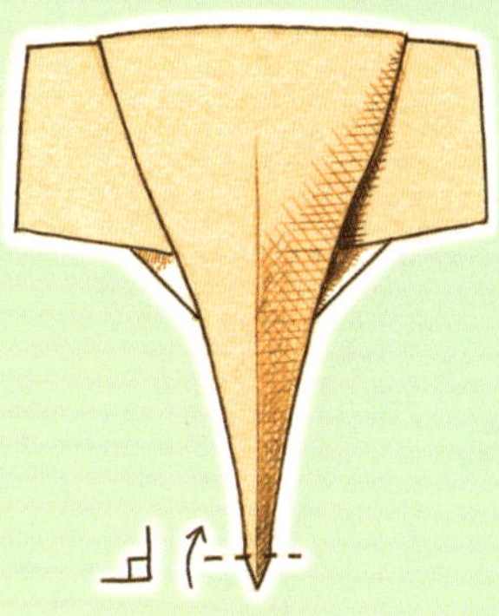

- 10 -

Fold the tip of the trunk up at a right angle, and continue to mold the shape by pinching it between your fingertips.

The finished model, brought to life. When shaping the trunk, you are aiming for neat pinches without unsightly creases, but this is easier said than done!

CICADA

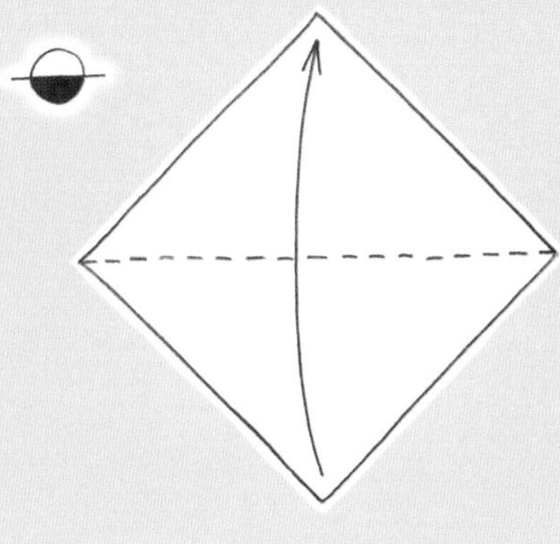

- 1 -

Position the paper as shown, fold in half from bottom to top to make a triangle.

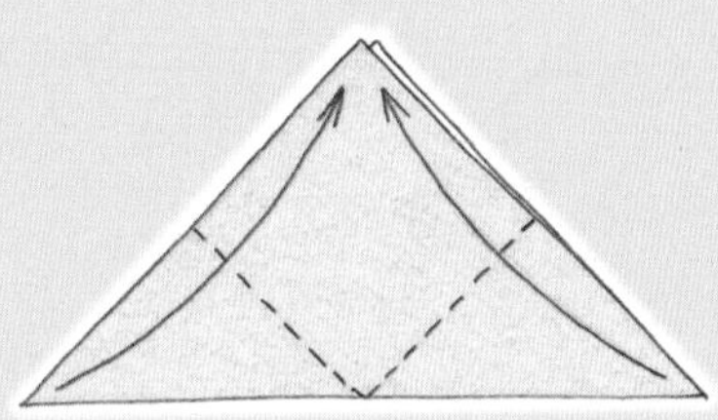

- 2 -

Fold the bottom corners upward.

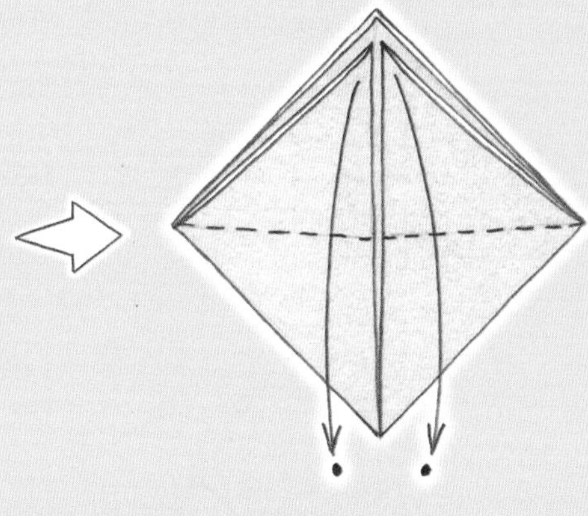

- 3 -

Fold these small flaps downward to each side, to sit just below and to the side of the bottom point as marked with dots.

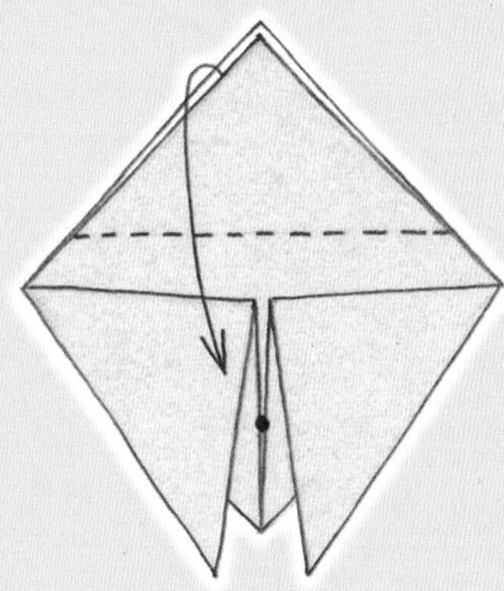

- 4 -

Fold the front flap at the top of the model downward as indicated, so the point meets the dot marked.

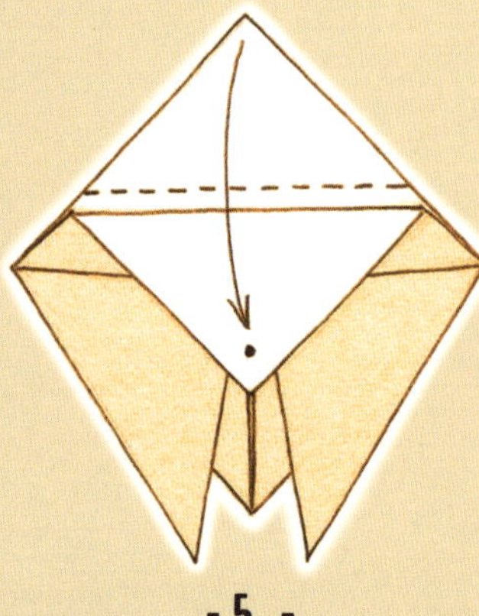

- 5 -

Fold the back flap at the top of the model downward as indicated, so the point meets the dot (on the reverse of the front flap).

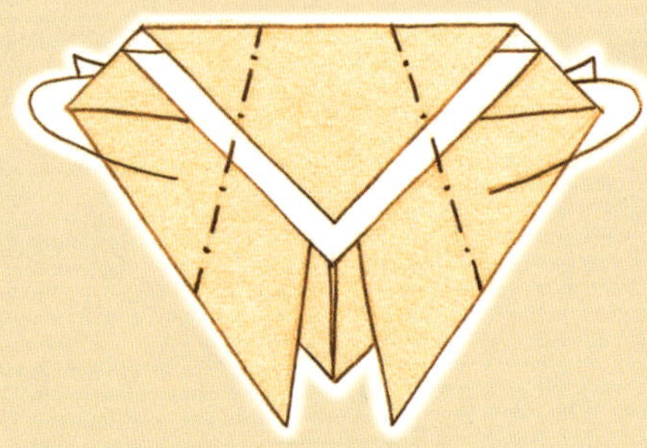

- 6 -

Fold each side to the back of the model, pressing the layers of the folds in place firmly.

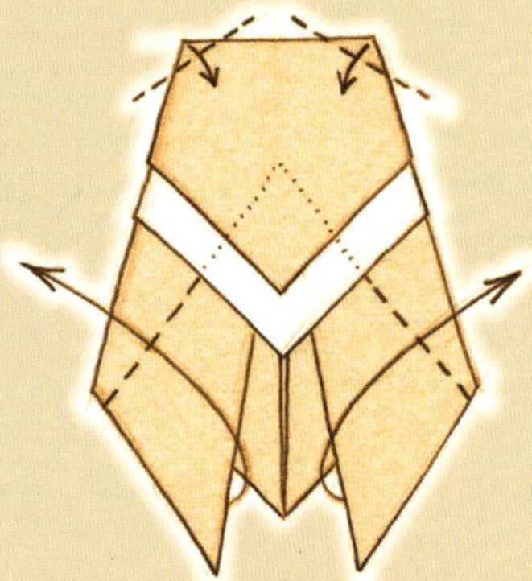

- 7 -

Fold top corners inward at a slight angle. Fold bottom flaps to each side – lift the 'pocket' to fold all the way up inside.

The finished model. The folds made in Step 7 form the eyes and the wings of the cicada.

BUTTERFLY

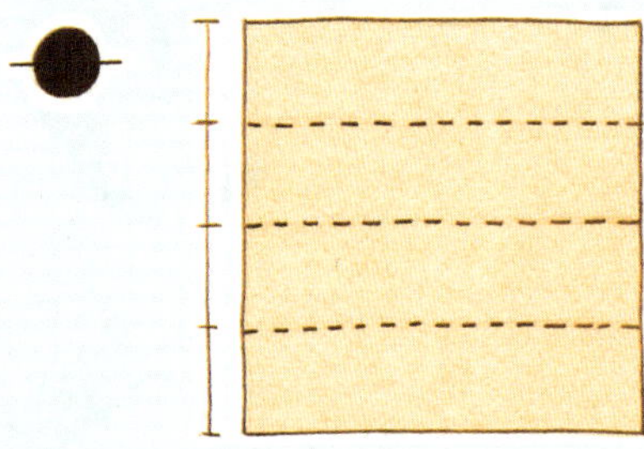

- 1 -

Fold the paper in half, then unfold to mark the center line. Fold the top and bottom edges to the center crease and unfold.

- 2 -

Your paper is now divided into four equal horizontal sections.

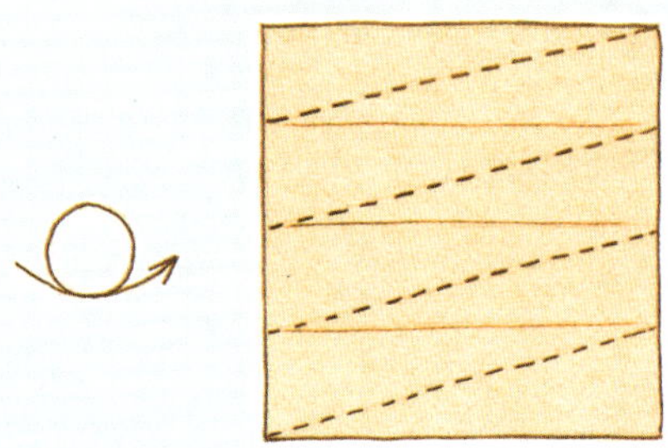

- 3 -

Turn it over. Make a diagonal fold across each segment – fold accuracy will determine the symmetry of your butterfly's wings.

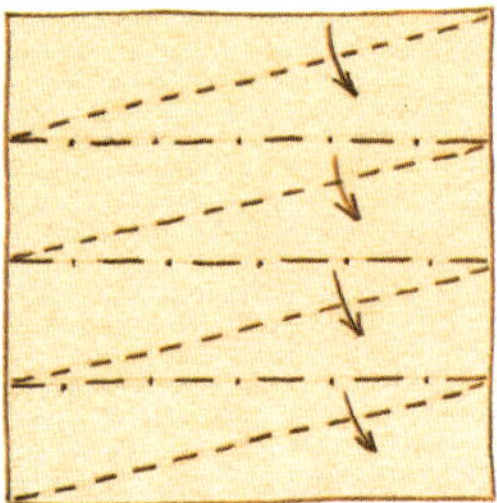

- 4 -

Gather up the folded segments.

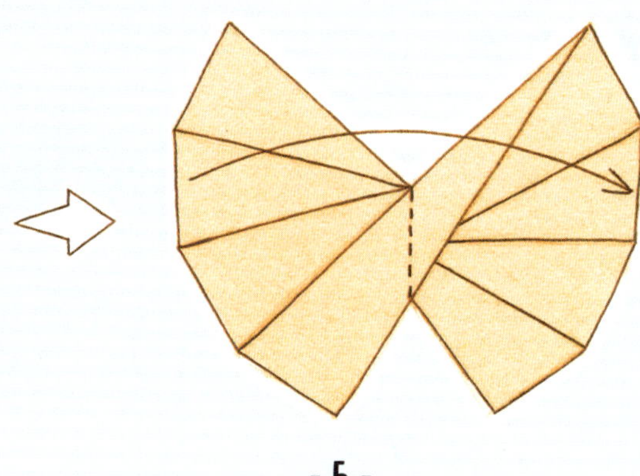

- 5 -

Your model should look like this. Fold in half so the edges of the wings meet.

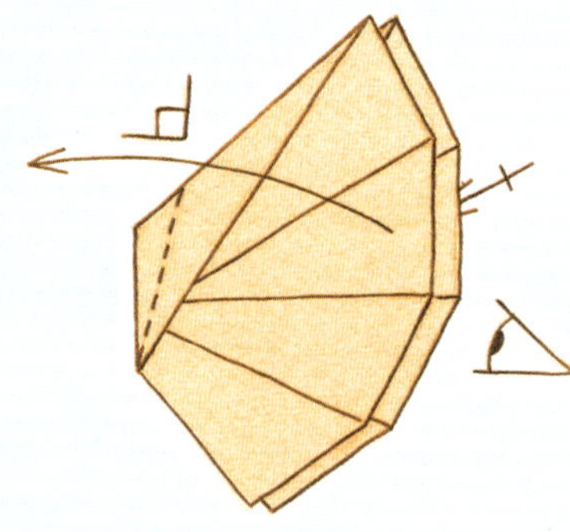

- 6 -

Fold the front wing back to make a diagonal fold at a right-angle. Repeat on the reverse side.

The folds made in Step 6 create the butterfly's body.

GOOSE

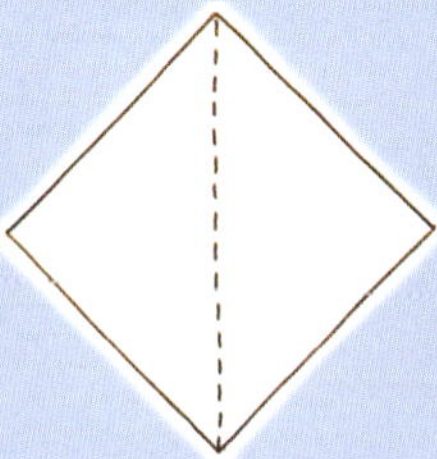

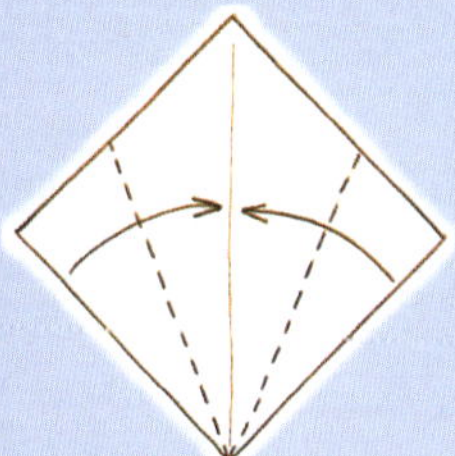

- 1 -

Position the paper as shown, fold in half from side to side then unfold.

- 2 -

Fold in each side to meet the center crease.

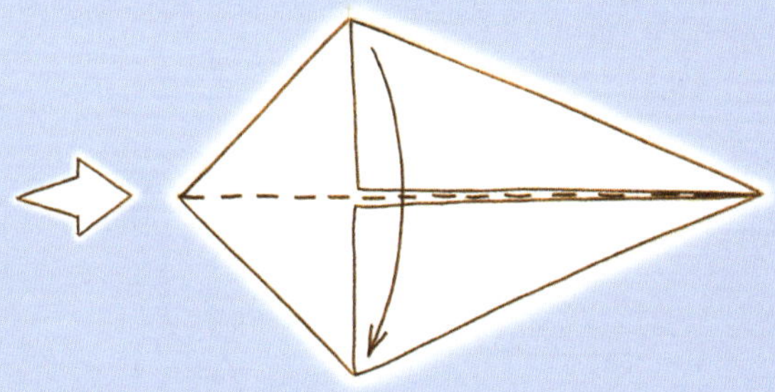

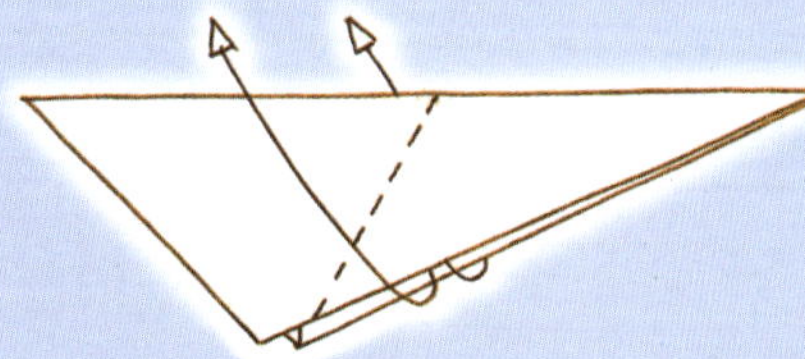

- 3 -

Turn the model onto its side and fold in half along the center crease.

- 4 -

Make an oblique fold, pressing firmly, then fold out the flaps as indicated, from the inside to the outside, and flatten to create the neck. Check the angle is as Step 5.

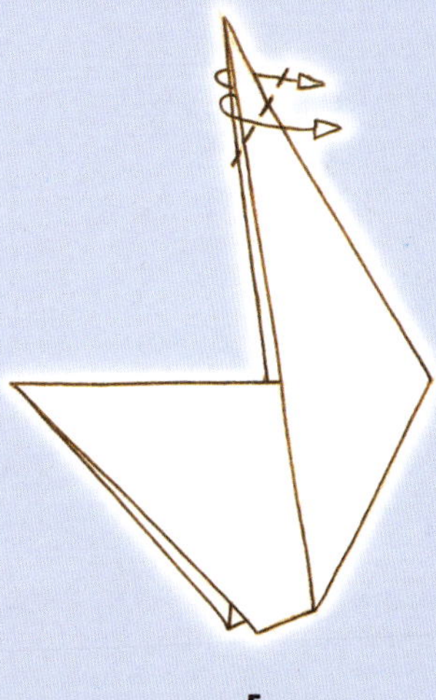

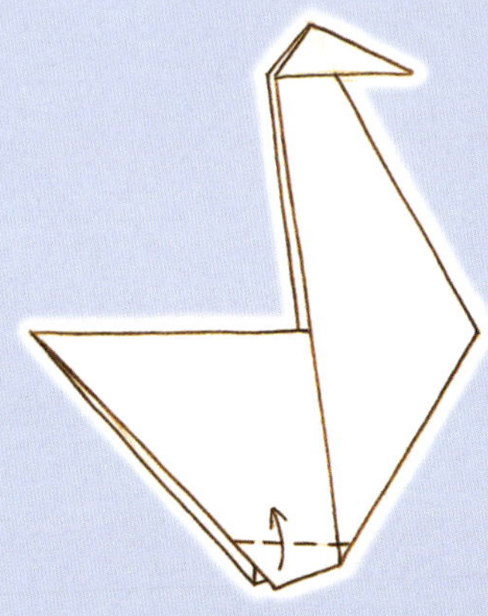

- 5 -

Make an oblique fold at the top point, then fold out the flaps from the inside to the outside and flatten to make the head.

- 6 -

Now to make the feet. Fold up the front flap at the bottom point.

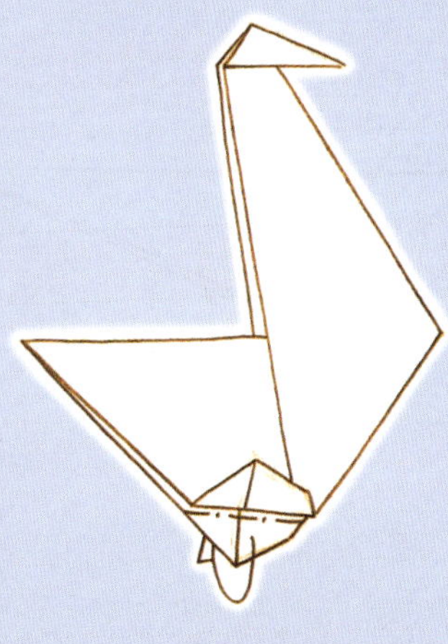

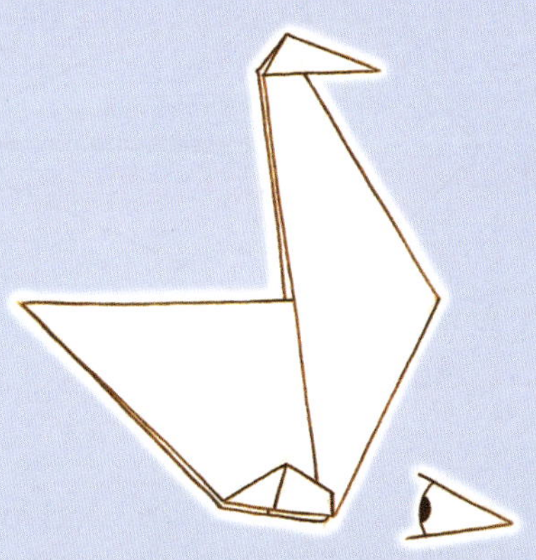

- 7 -

Then fold up the back flap to the back.

- 8 -

Now let's change our view of the feet.

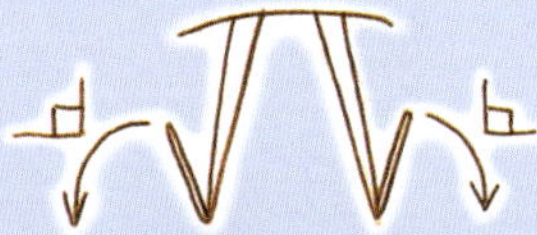

- 9 -

Turning the model so the beak is facing you, fold down each flap at the base to make right-angle folds.

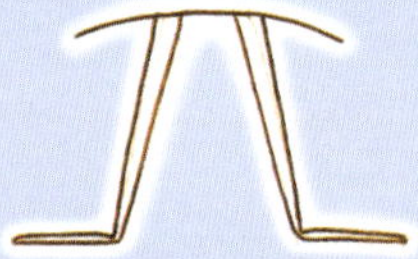

- 10 -

The feet should support the weight of your model, if the angle of the neck is correct.

The finished goose should be nice and stable. If the angle of the neck fold in Step 4 is wrong, it may topple over!

MONKEY

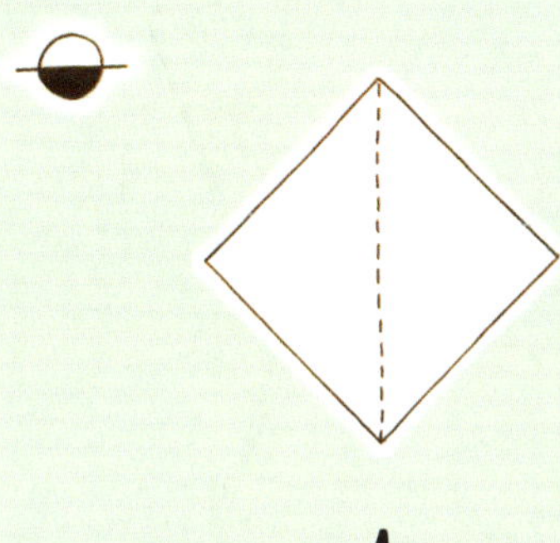

- 1 -

Position the paper as shown, fold in half from side to side then unfold.

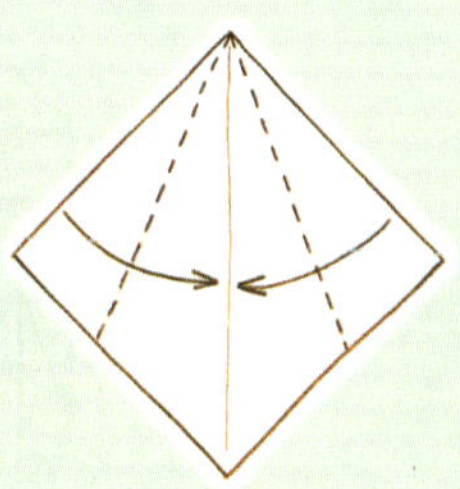

- 2 -

Fold in each side to meet the center crease.

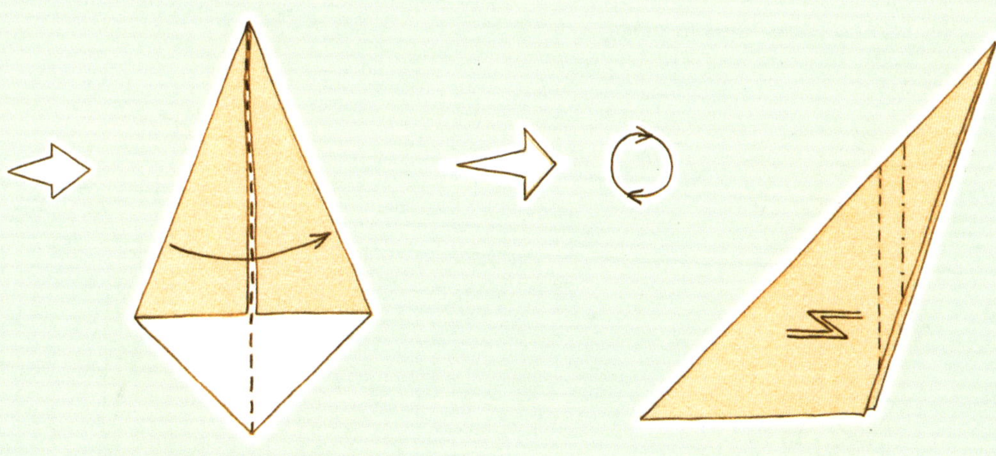

- 3 -

Fold in half along the center crease.

- 4 -

Make a pleat fold through both layers of the paper.

- 5 -

Mark middle of top flap with a mountain fold and unfold. Press down on the top edge to flatten and press folds in place.

- 6 -

To start to shape the face, fold a pleat fold through the top layer only of the head flap.

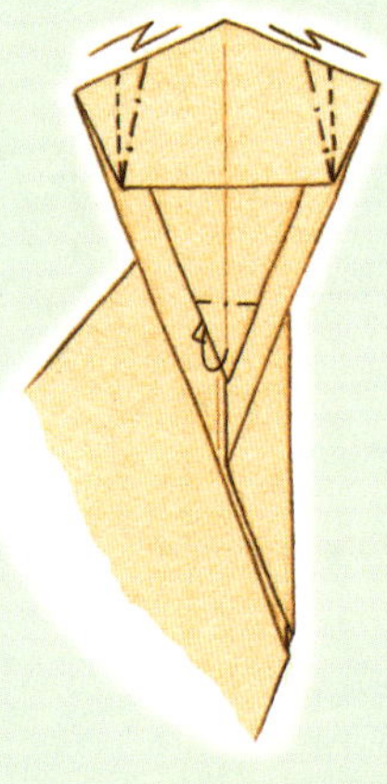

- 7 -

Make pleat folds for the ears and fold under the flap at the base of the head.

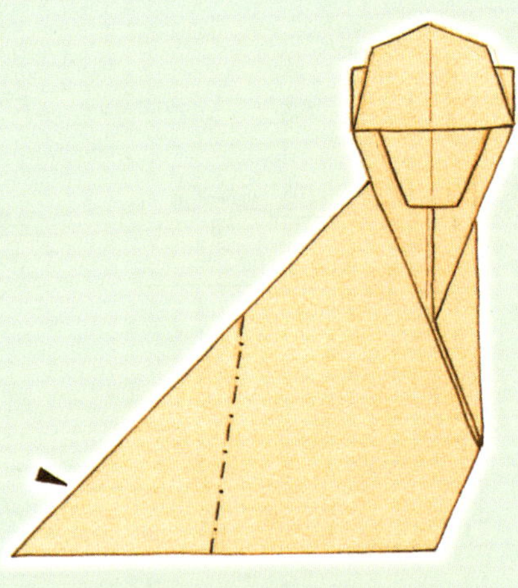

- 8 -

To start the tail, press as marked to make a fold to the inside.

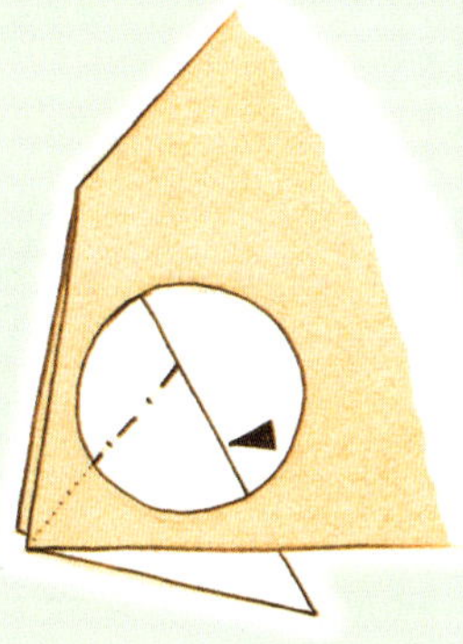

- 9 -

Press inside where marked (see cutaway for interior view) to push the fold to the outside.

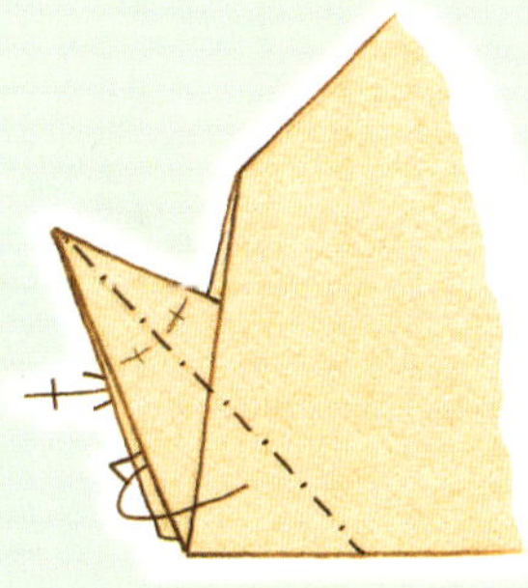

- 10 -

Fold the front flap of the tail to the inside of the model, and repeat to the back.

The pleat fold made in Step 6 is instrumental in creating the monkey's hooded visage.

SEAL

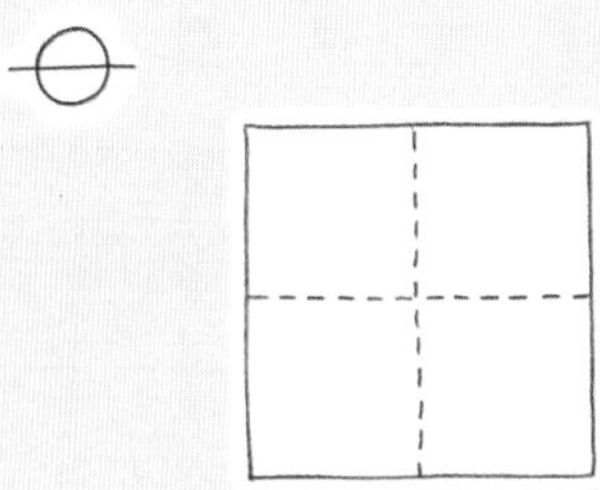

- 1 -

Fold and unfold the paper vertically and horizontally.

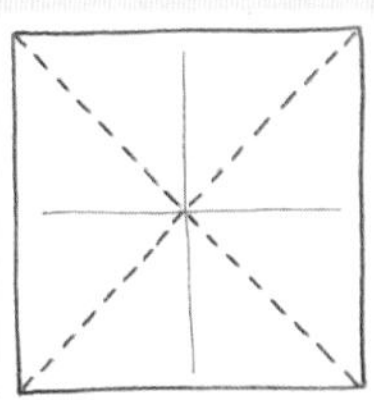

- 2 -

Fold and unfold along both diagonals.

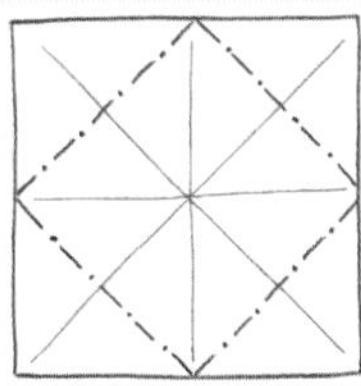

- 3 -

Fold each corner to the center with a mountain fold, unfolding each time.

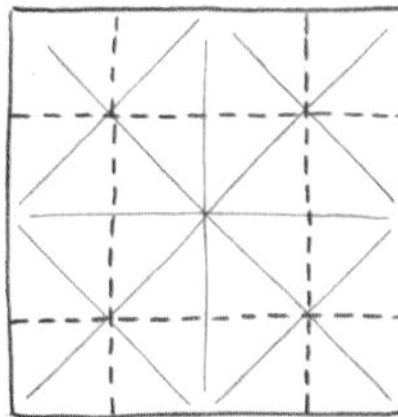

- 4 -

Fold each side to the center with a valley fold, unfolding each time.

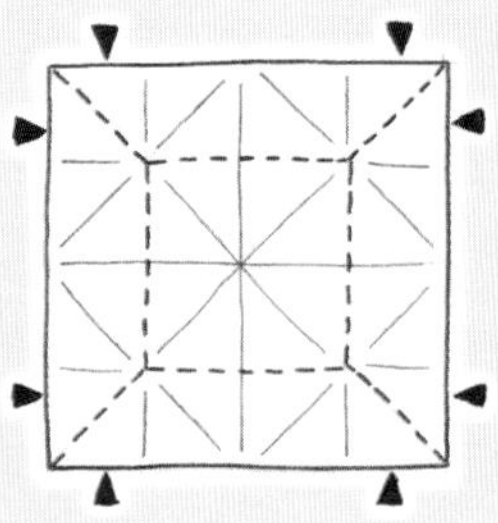

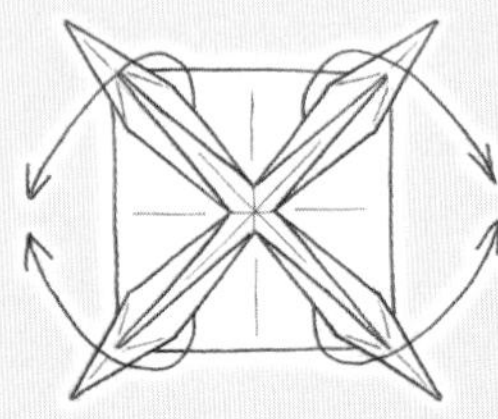

- 5 -

Pinching at each corner as marked...

- 6 -

...start to fold the pinched corners to the outside...

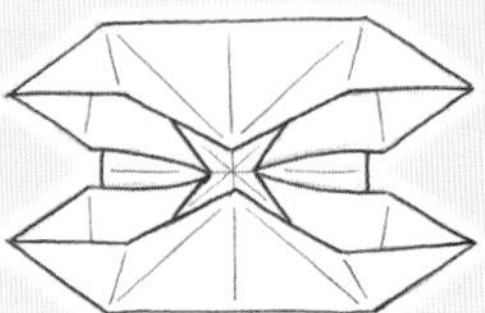

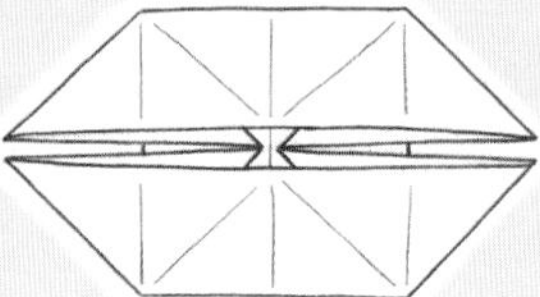

- 7 -

...flattening them as you go.

- 8 -

Your model now looks like this.

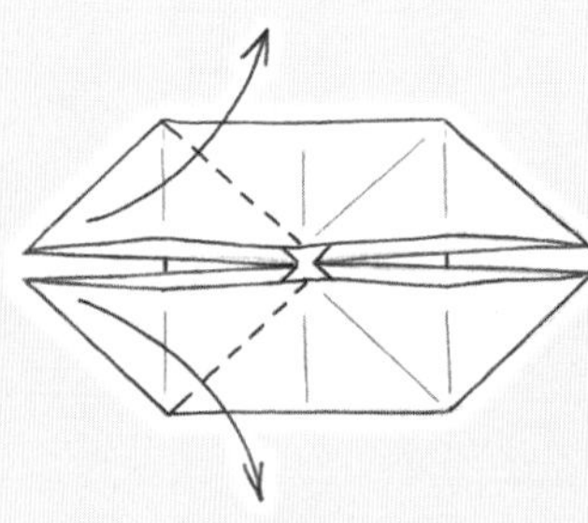

- 9 -

Fold in the left-hand flaps as shown.

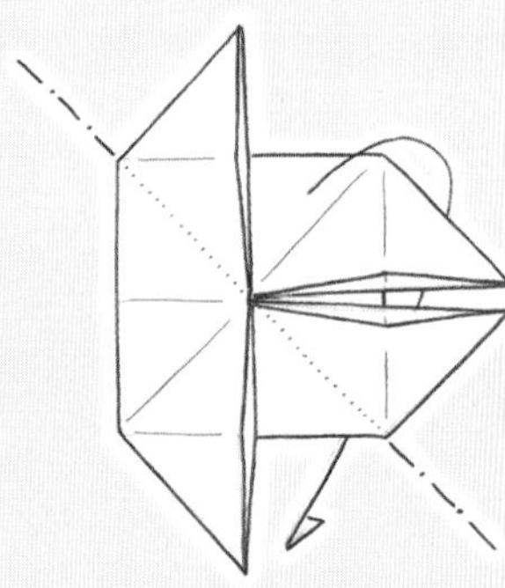

- 10 -

Fold the top right-hand flap to the back to meet the bottom left-hand flap.

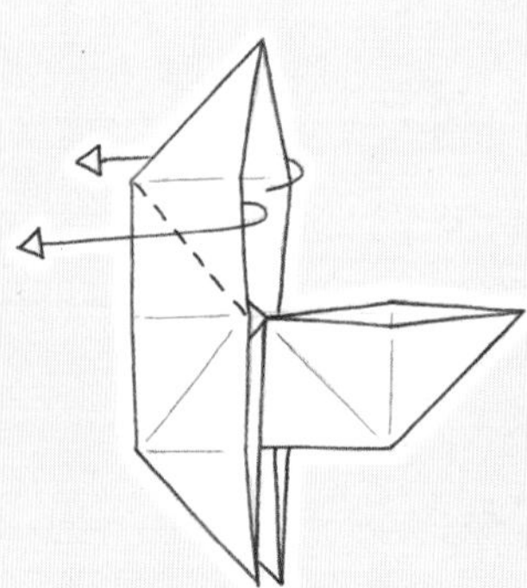

- 11 -

Bring the inside of the top flap to the outside (slightly unfold the top of the model to do this), and flatten to make the seal's head.

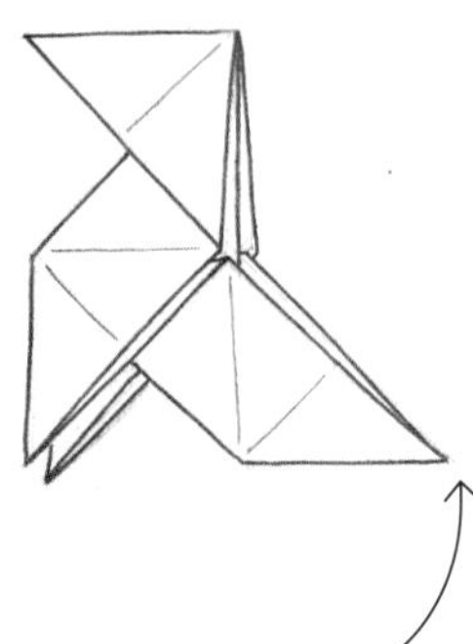

Bring the tail of the seal down to sit the finished model on the work surface.

SNAIL

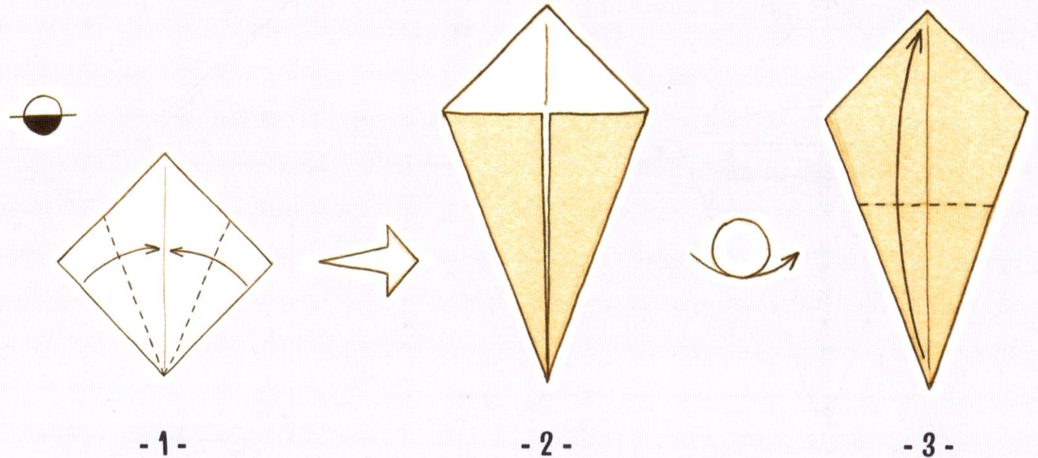

- 1 -

Position the paper as shown, fold in half from side to side then unfold.

- 2 -

Fold in each side to meet the center crease.

- 3 -

Turn the model over and fold in half from bottom to top.

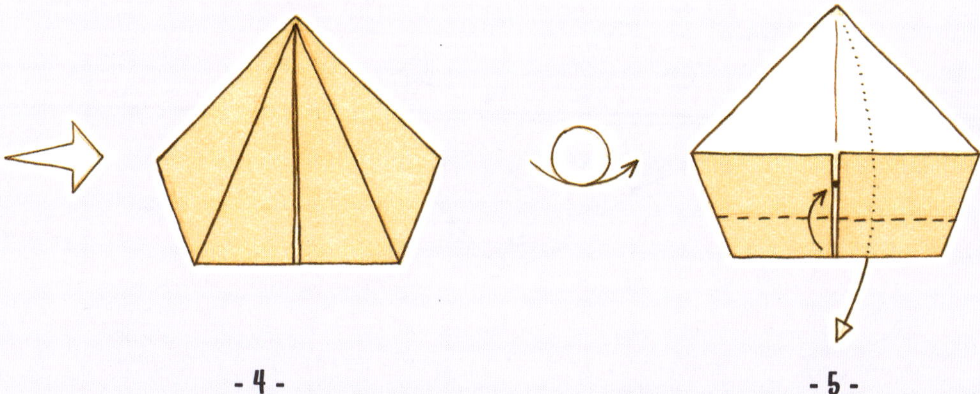

- 4 -

Your model now looks like this. Turn it over.

- 5 -

Fold the back flap down from behind, so that the existing fold meets the marked dot (see Step 6 for how this looks).

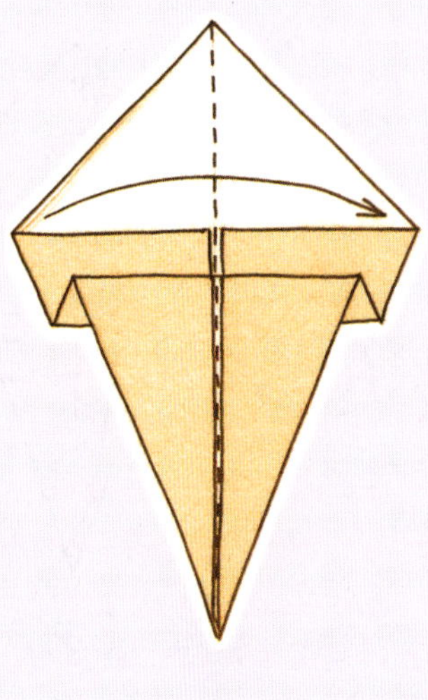

- 6 -

Fold in half along the center crease.

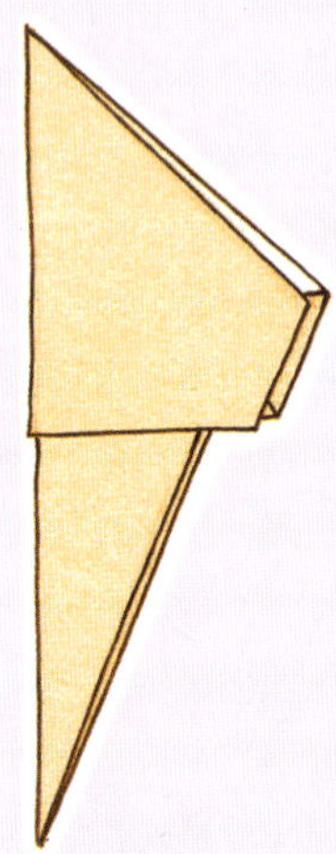

- 7 -

Your model now looks like this. Rotate by 90 degrees to the right.

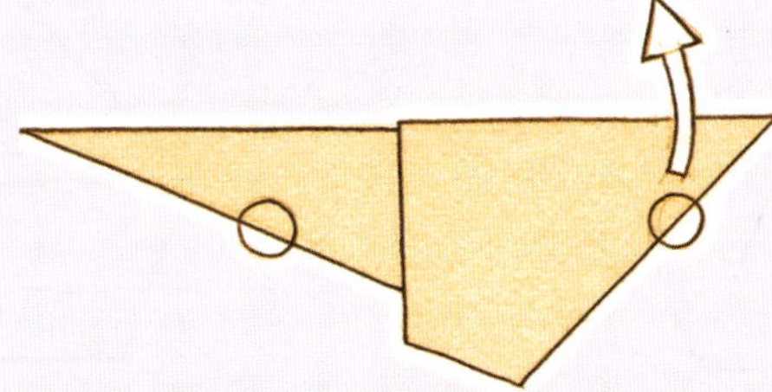

- 8 -

Hold model as indicated and pull up in the direction of the arrow to reveal the hidden fold at the base. Flatten the folds.

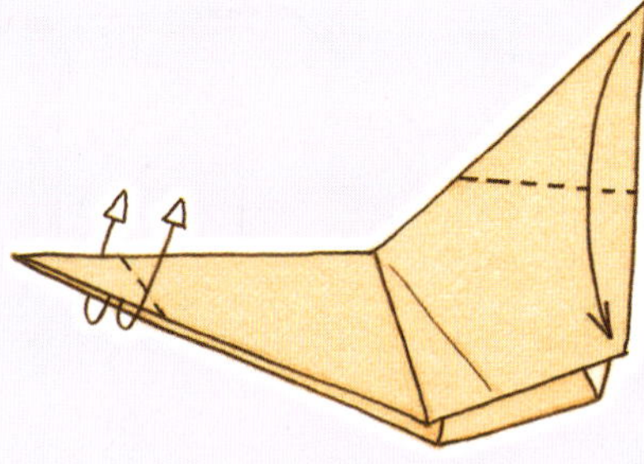

- 9 -

Fold left-hand tip as indicated, then slightly open the model at this point to fold each flap backward to make the snail's head. Fold the right-hand flap down as indicated.

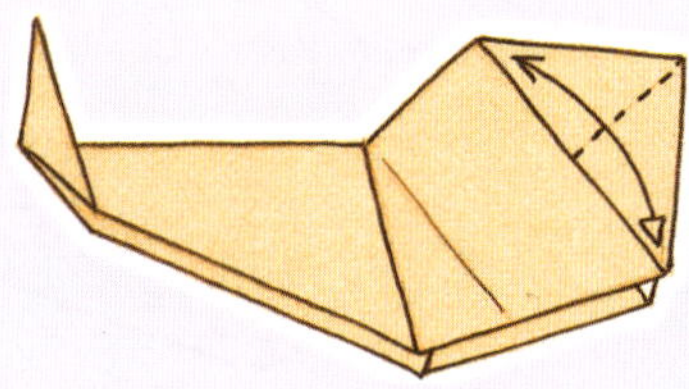

- 10 -

Fold the right-hand flap back on itself as indicated, then unfold.

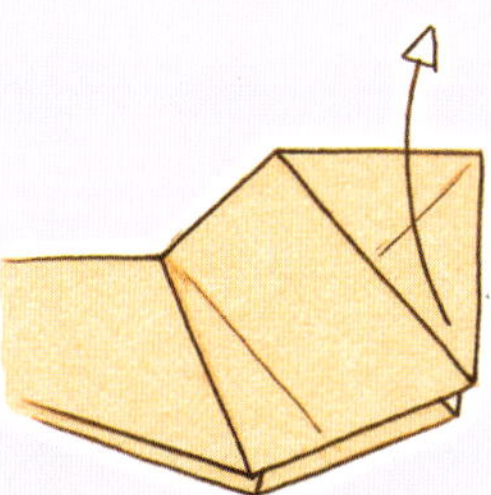

- 11 -

Unfold the right-hand flap so it is pointing straight up (see Step 12).

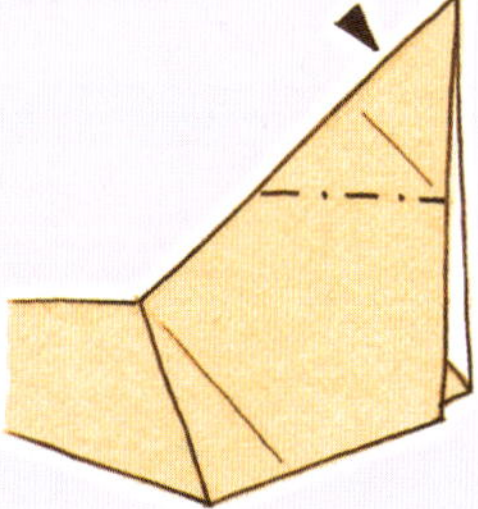

- 12 -

Press the marked point inward, and press firmly along the indicated line.

- 13 -

The shell-end of your model now looks like this.

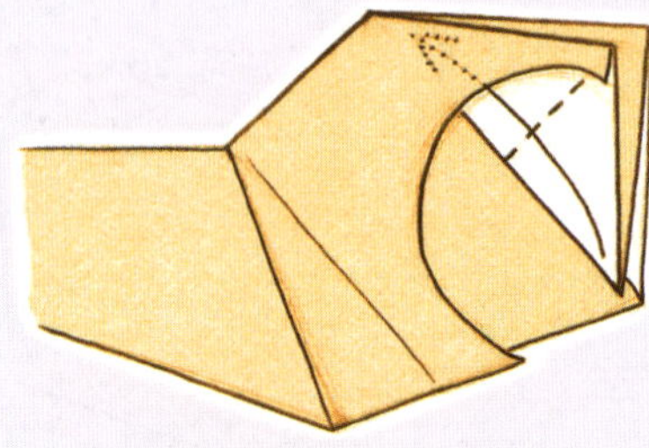

- 14 -

Fold the inner flap back along the indicated line (see cutaway for interior view).

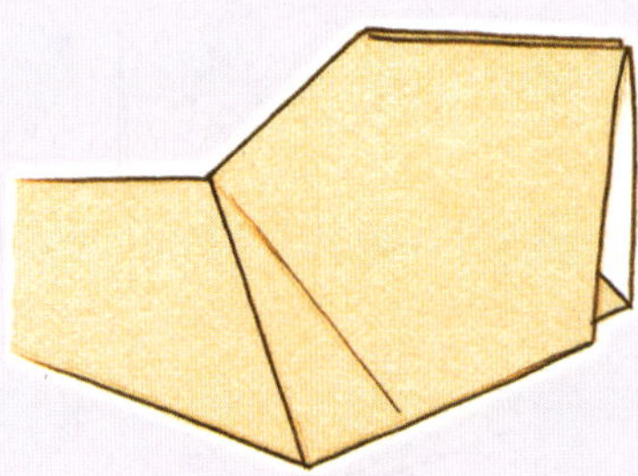

- 15 -

This securely locks the snail shell in place.

FROG

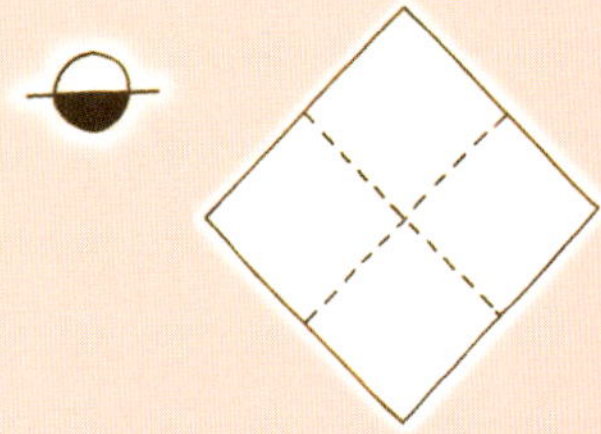

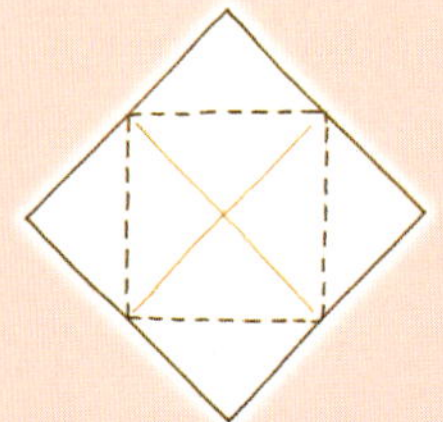

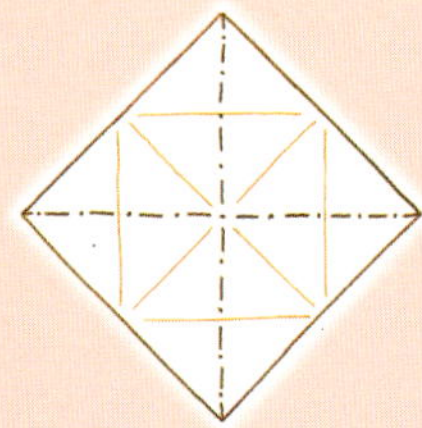

- 1 -

Fold and unfold the paper vertically and horizontally, then position as shown.

- 2 -

Fold each point to the center then unfold.

- 3 -

Fold in half bottom to top with a mountain fold and repeat from side to side.

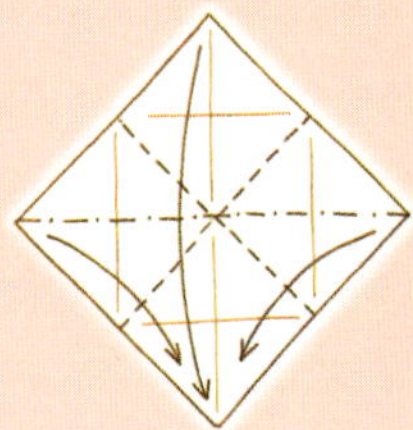

- 4 -

Fold in the sides to meet the bottom point, and you'll find that the top point starts to fold down too. Flatten the folds.

- 5 -

Your model now looks like this.

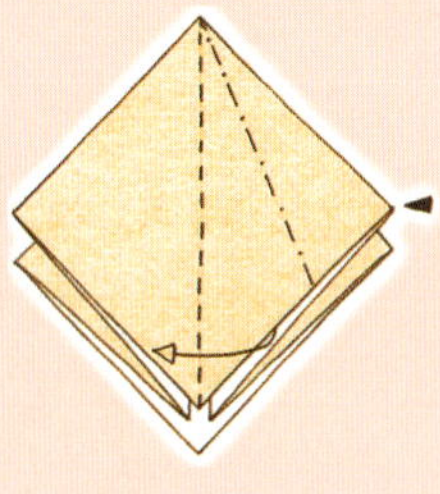

- 6 -

Fold over the top flap as you press in on the side point as marked and flatten the fold to the center.

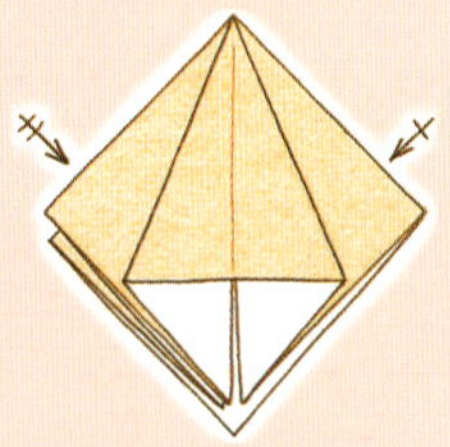

- 7 -

Your model now looks like this. Repeat the fold in Step 6 on each of the flaps behind.

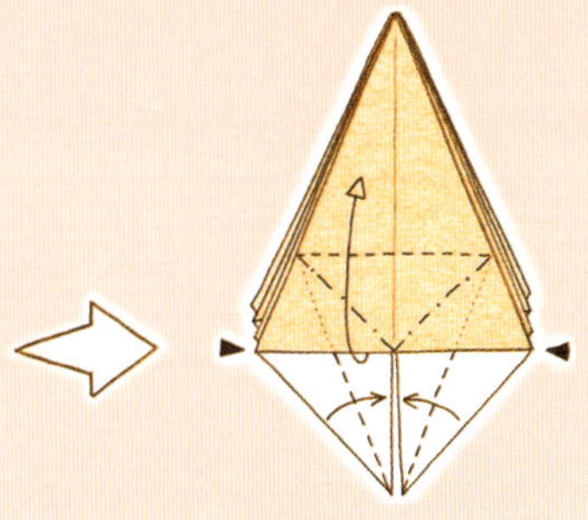

- 8 -

Fold sides of top layer to the center, then unfold. Push in at the sides as marked, while bringing the center point up; flatten the fold.

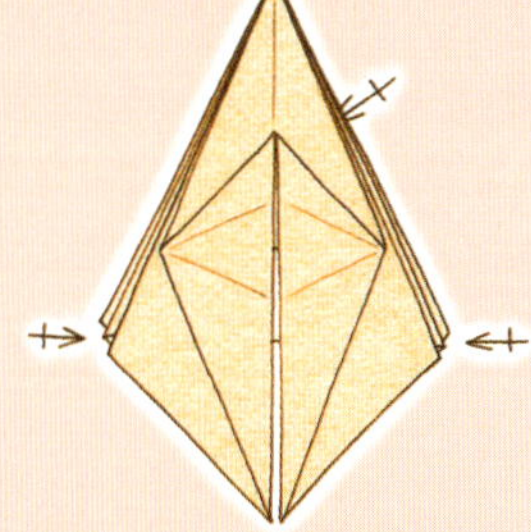

- 9 -

Your model now looks like this. Repeat the fold in Step 8 on each of the flaps behind.

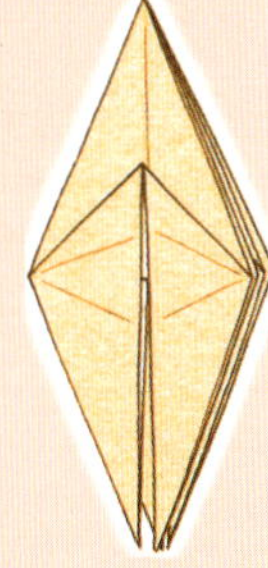

- 10 -

Your model now looks like this.

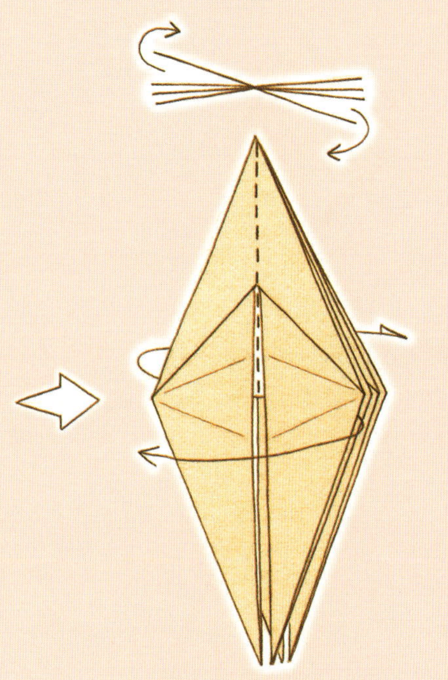

- 11 -

Fold the top and back flaps over as shown, making sure you have the same number of layers on each side of the model.

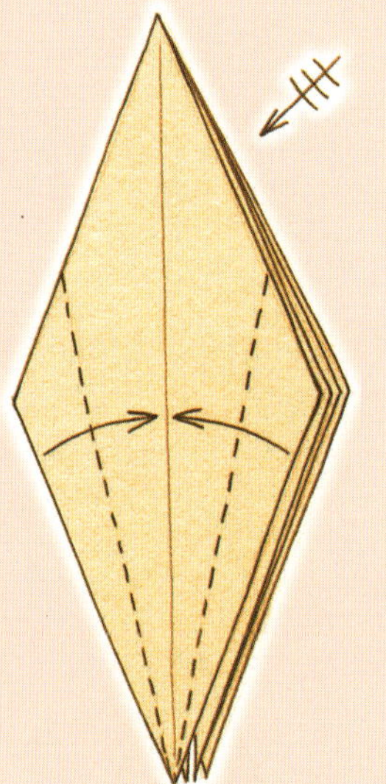

- 12 -

Your model now looks like this. Fold in the sides to the center of the top flap as shown, then repeat on each of the flaps behind.

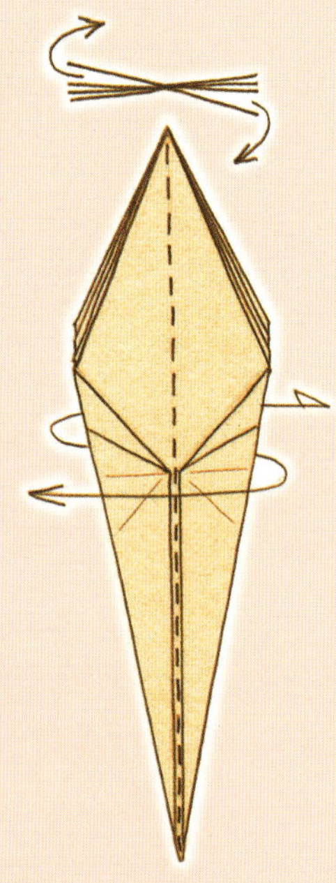

- 13 -

Your model now looks like this. Fold top and back flaps over making sure you have the same number of layers on each side of the model.

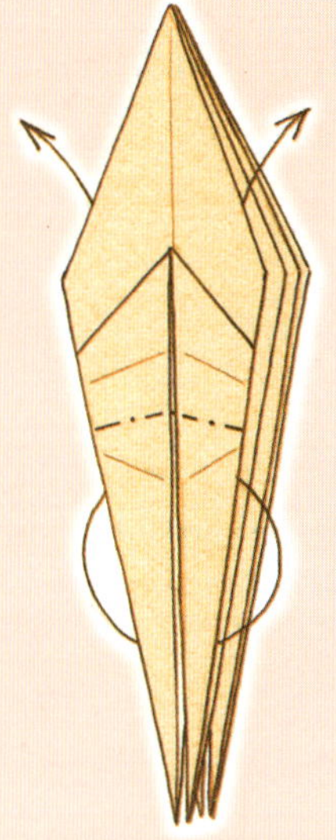

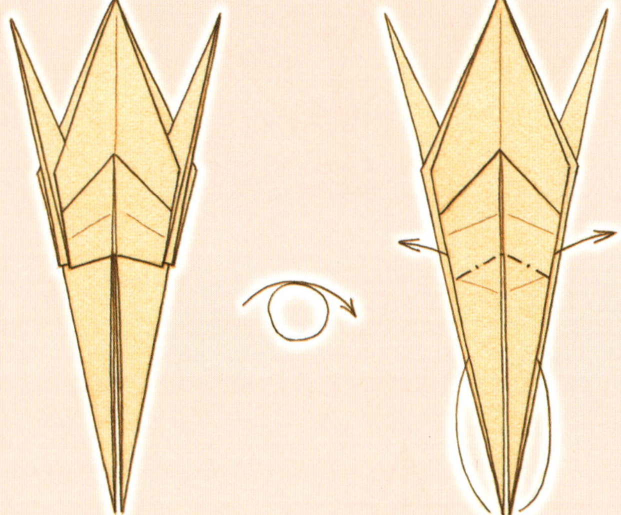

- 14 -

Your model now looks like this. Fold back the 'forelegs' to lie between the layers of the upper flap.

- 15 -

Your model now looks like this. Turn it over.

- 16 -

Now to make the hind legs. Fold back each leg to sit between the flap layers.

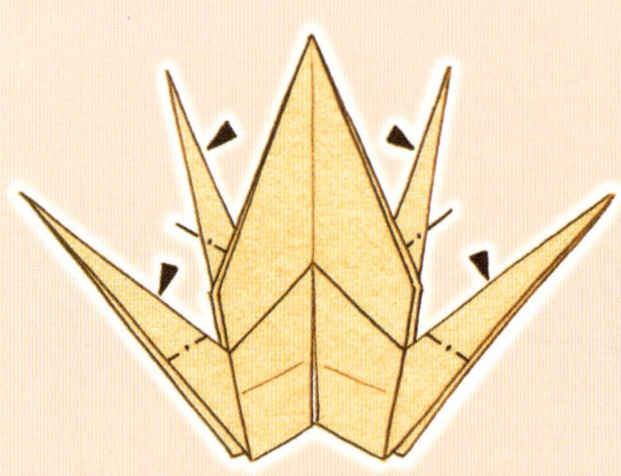

- 17 -

Fold the forelegs and hind legs as shown, then press at the marked points to give dimension to the limbs.

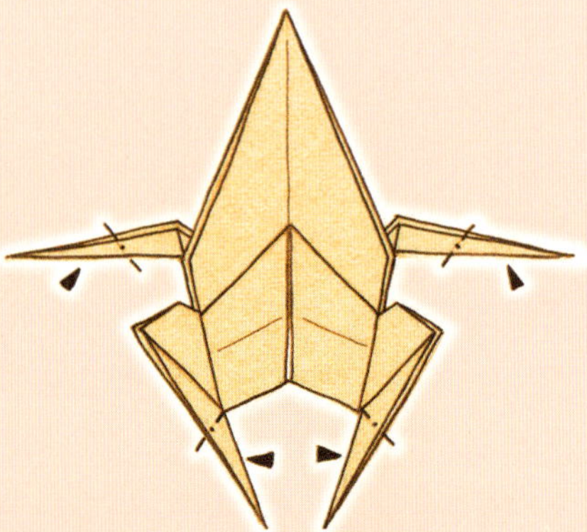

- 18 -

Repeat as marked to further refine the shaping of the legs.

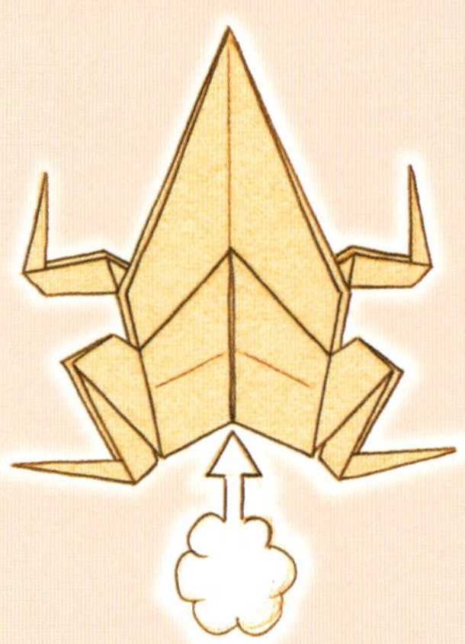

- 19 -

Blow into the base of the frog to inflate the body.

The inflated frog has a nicely rounded shape.

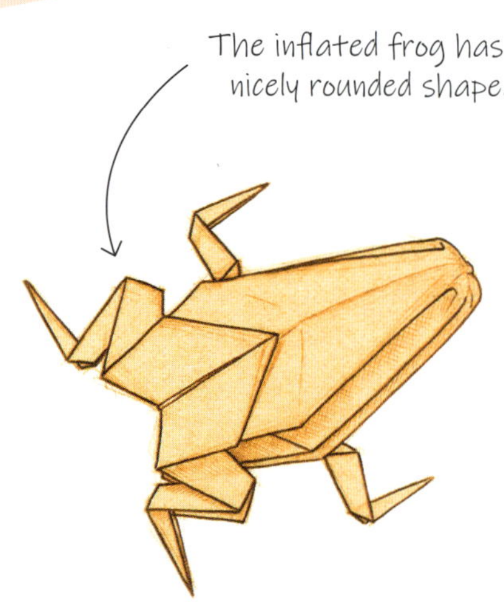

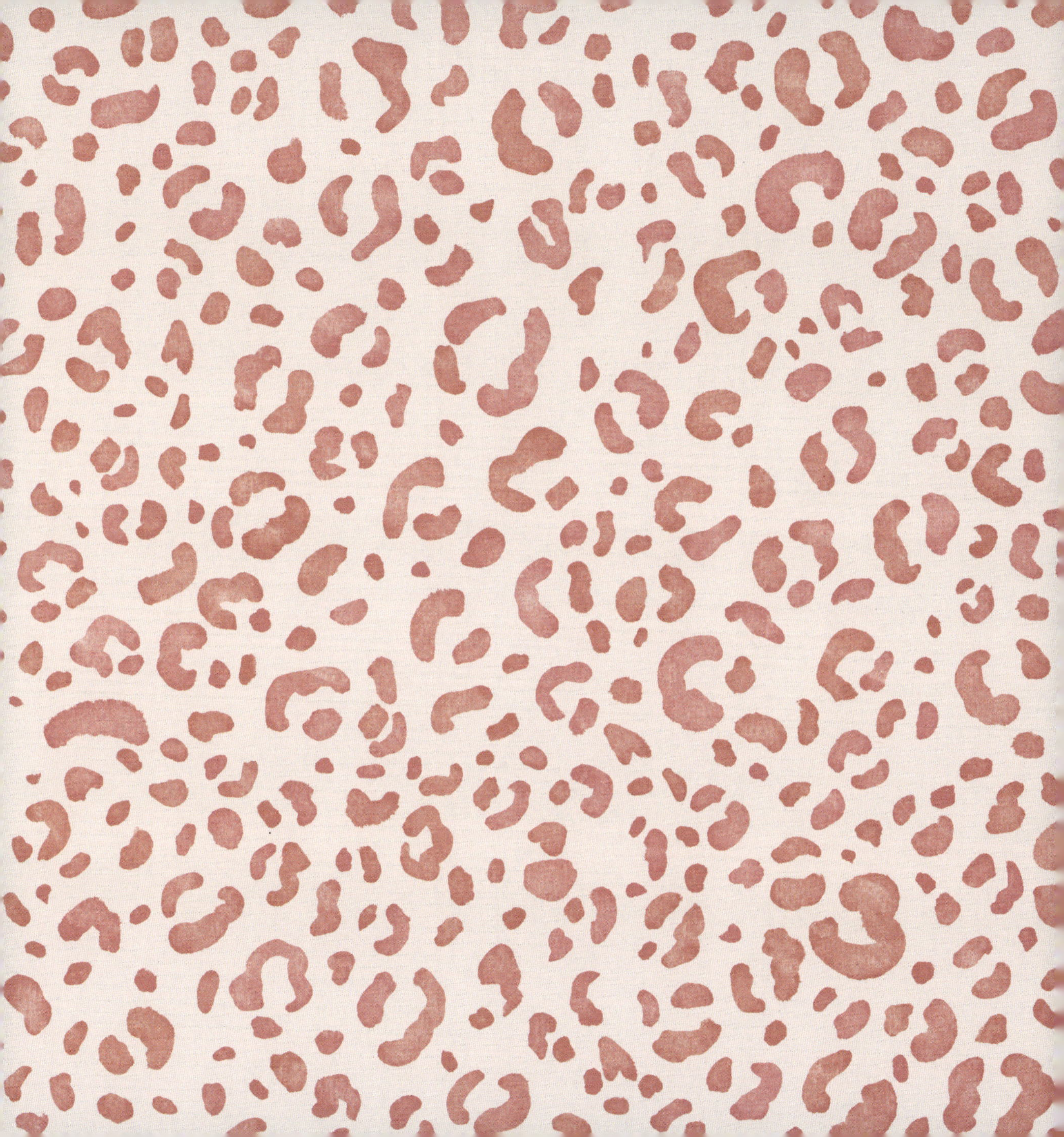

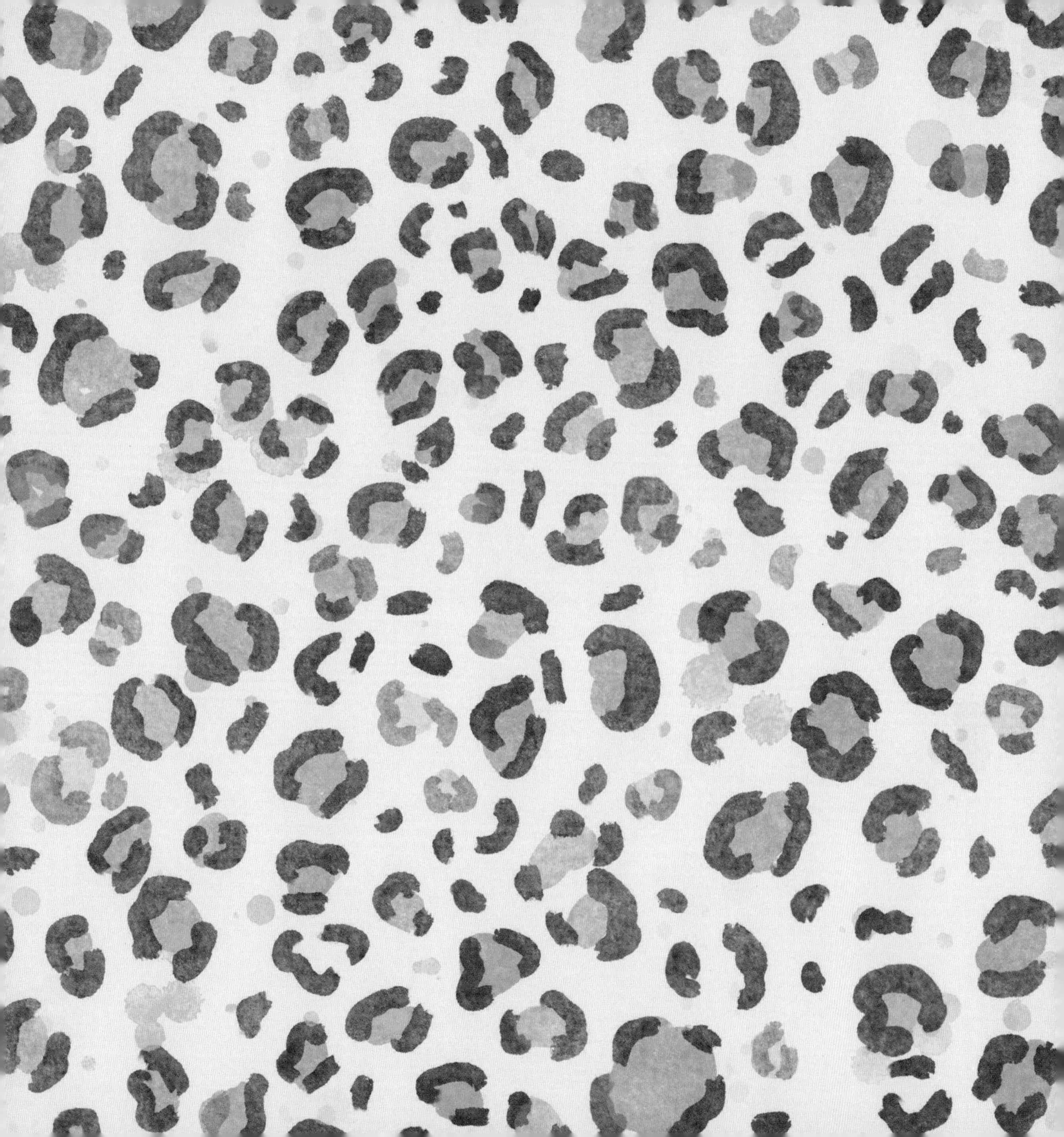

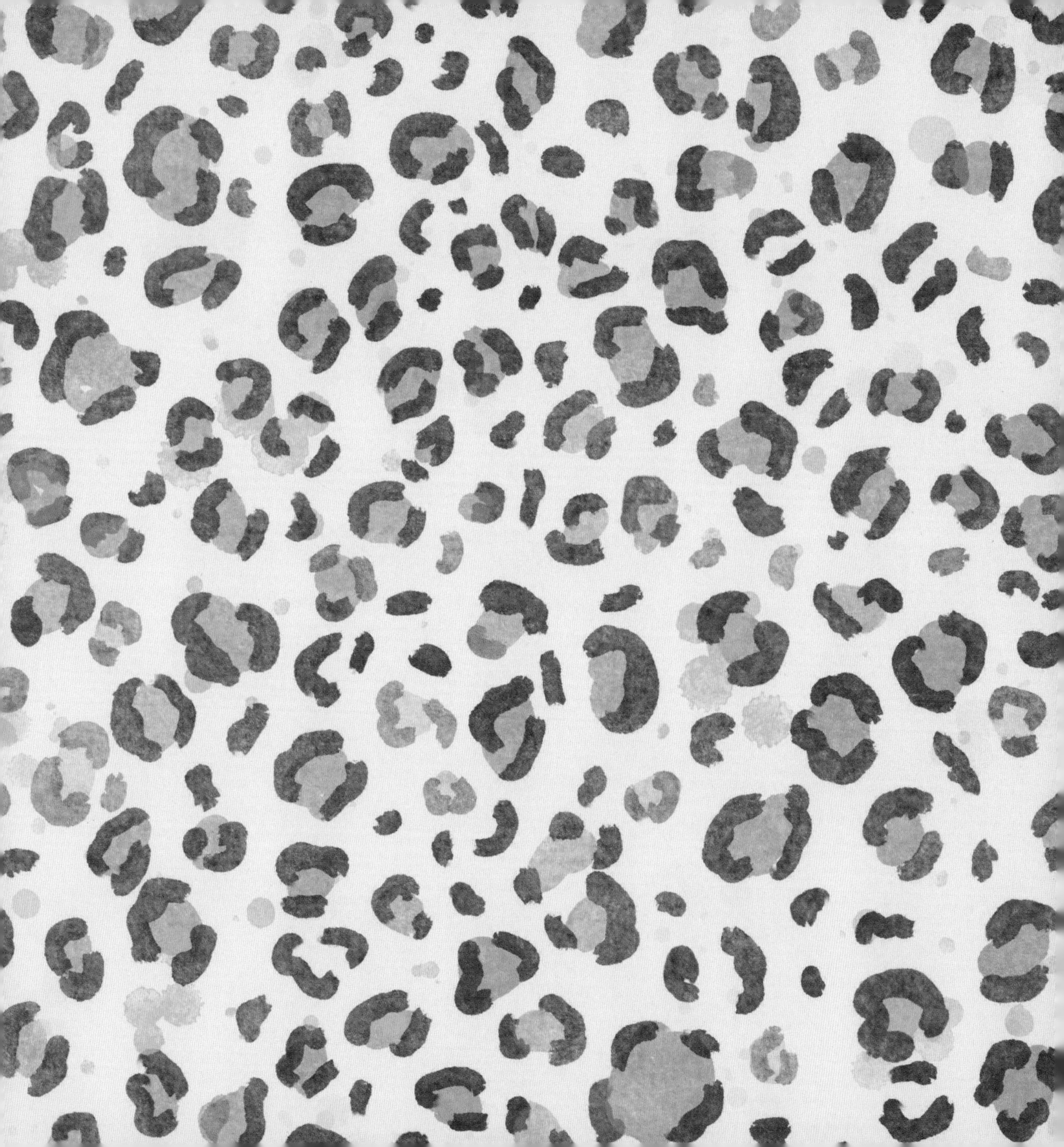

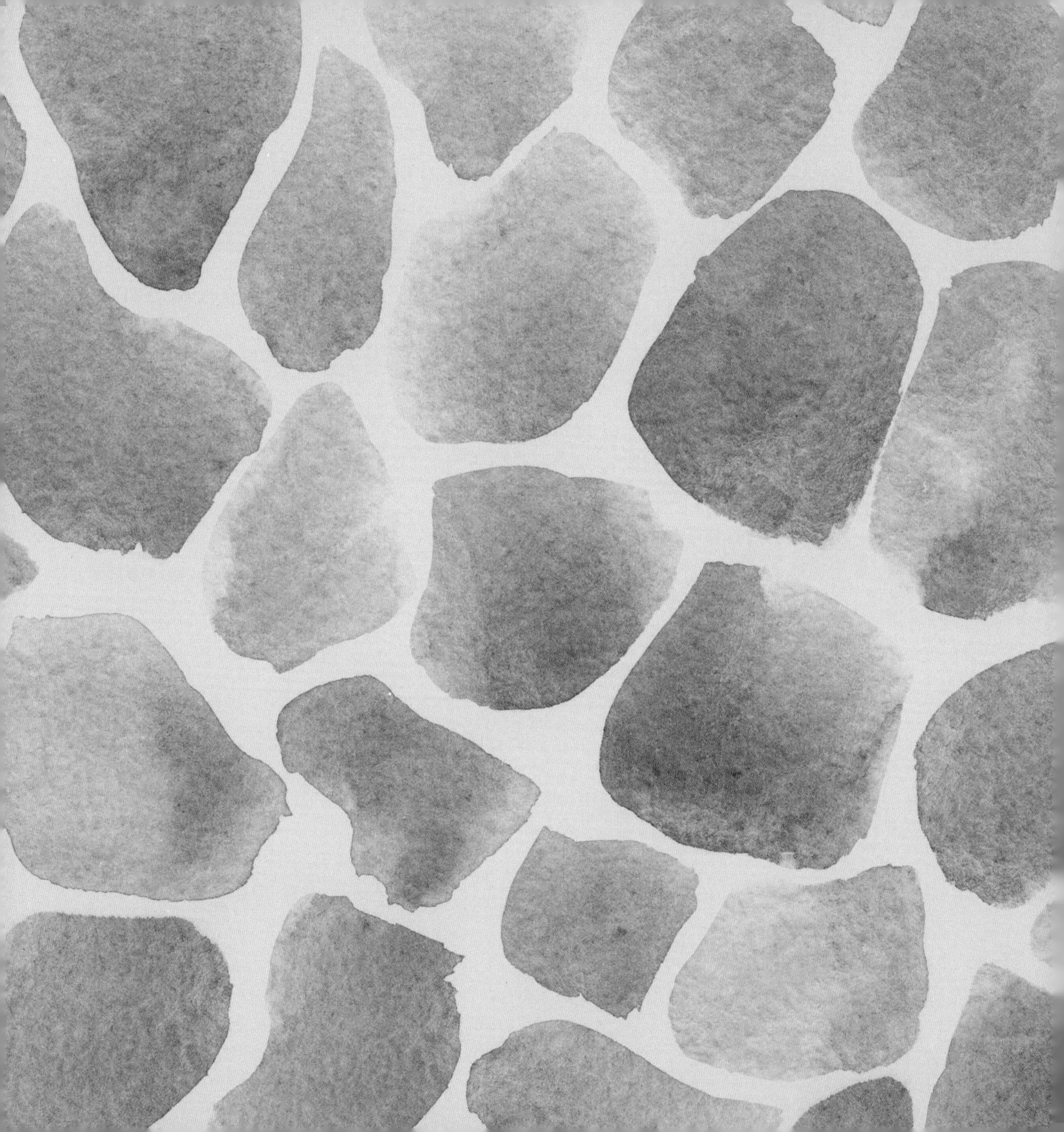

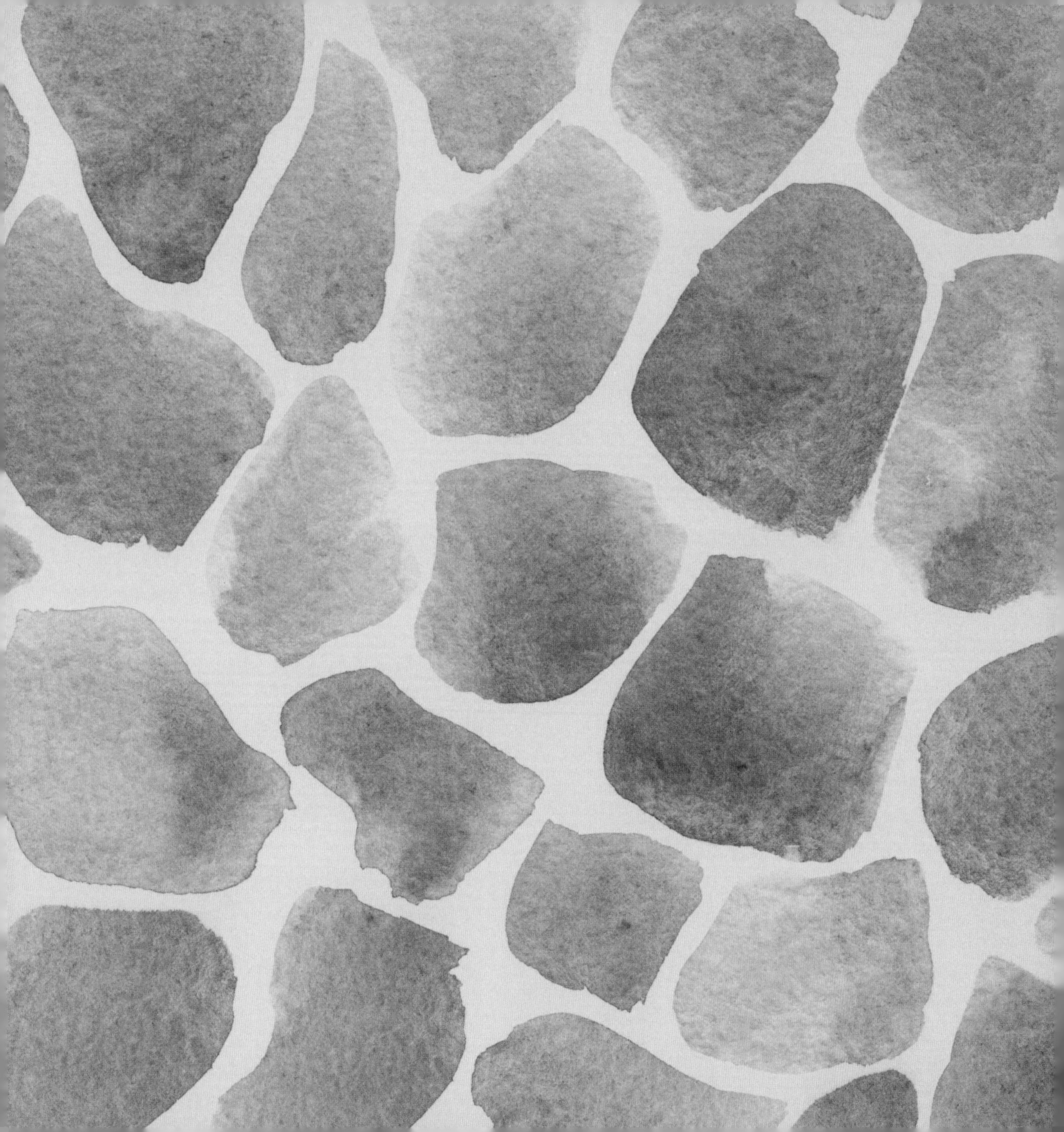

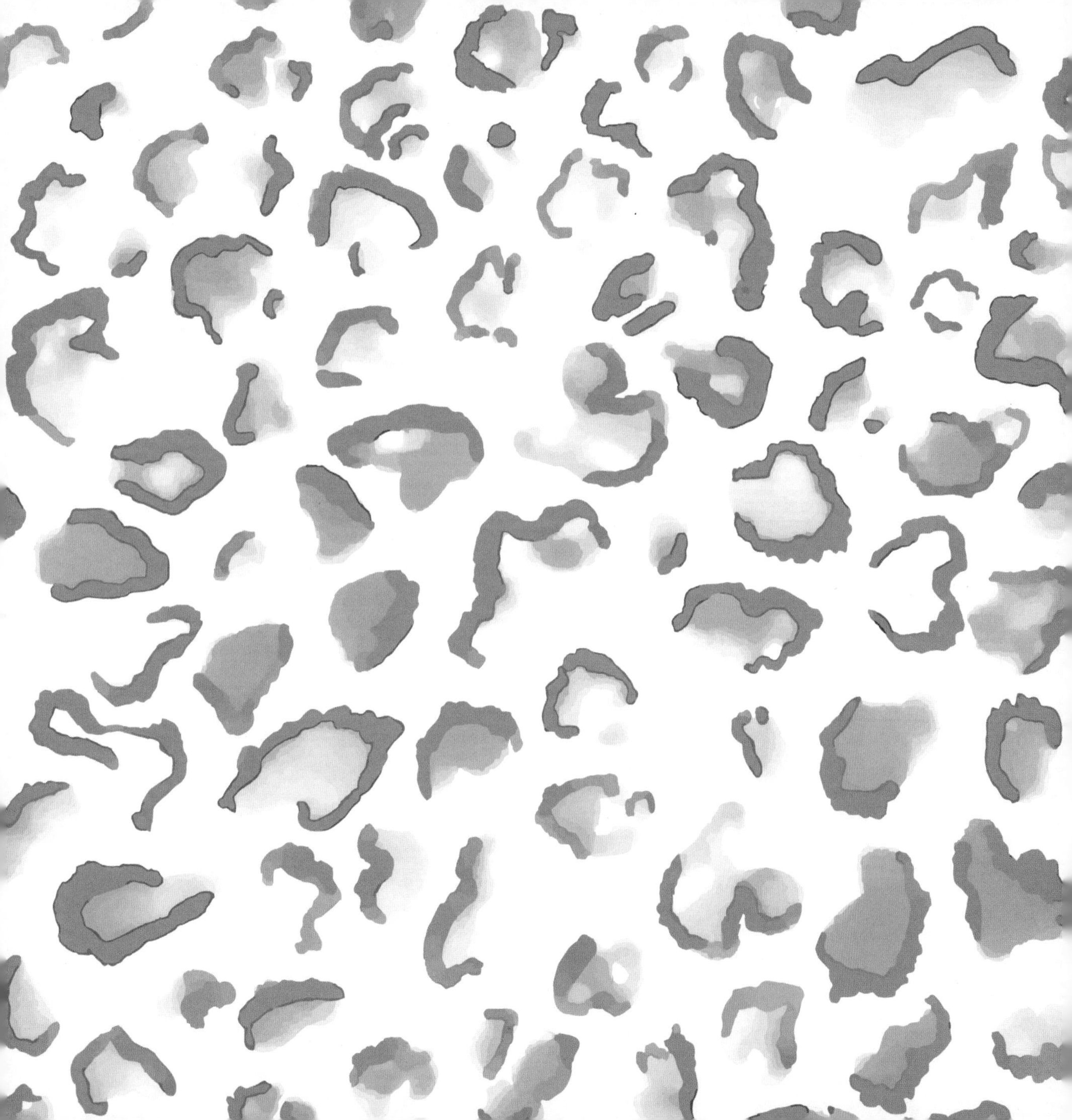

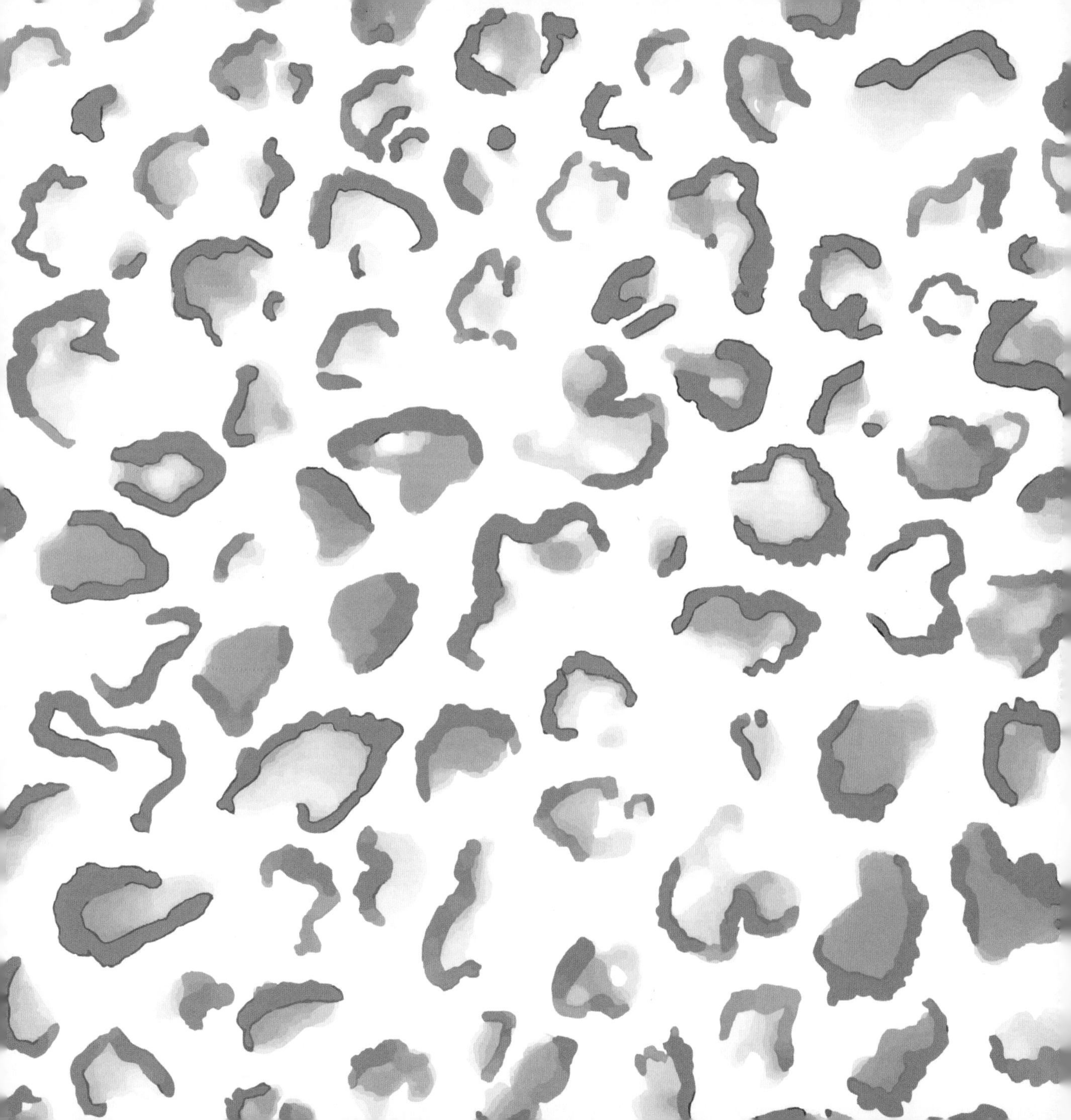